Inspiring Native American Stories for Kids

Captivating Tales of Tradition, Wisdom, and Resilience to Nurture Cultural Appreciation and Empathy

Table of Contents

Introduction

Ever since the first people gathered around fires, storytelling has been a way to share the highs and lows of life with family and friends. Long ago, people learned important lessons when life was tough with wild hunts and deep connections to nature. They turned these lessons into amazing myths and stories about big beasts, powerful gods, and mysterious spirits. These stories have been passed down from parents to kids for thousands of years; now, you can read them, too!

The Native Americans have always felt a special bond with the earth, the air, and the bright sun. Their unique way of seeing the world comes from their smart ways, strong hearts, and old traditions. These stories are filled with adventures and lessons from the past that still matter today. As you read, you'll feel like you're part of the action, meeting brave heroes and magical creatures along the way.

Imagine reading these stories by a campfire, the air filled with the smell of s'mores and the sounds of crickets and rustling trees—it's the perfect setting for tales that are exciting and a bit spooky. Or read them at bedtime and let your dreams be adventures. These stories will stick with you forever, teaching you about the magic of nature, the strength of sticking together, the bravery of heroes, and the hope for a better future.

As you dive into this book, you'll connect with the wisdom of many different Native American tribes. Picture yourself in their thrilling tales of adventure and bravery, meeting wise chiefs, magical animals, and fearless warriors. Discover secrets and wonders that time almost forgot.

These ancient American traditions are just waiting for you to explore. Get ready for a thrilling journey into history with each page you turn!

Chapter 1: Stories of the Ancestors: Timeless Legends

What Is Native American Folklore?

Folklore is the stories and customs passed down from generation to generation.
https://pixabay.com/illustrations/fantasy-unicorn-rainbow-pegasus-7457387/

Folklore is the stories and customs that get passed down from generation to generation. Some stories are so old that it is difficult to tell where they came from. They sit so deep in the souls of people that it is impossible to separate these stories from a culture. What makes people different from all the animals on earth is their ability to tell stories and pass them on to their children. Folklore is created when many people keep passing on a tradition so much that it becomes a part of who they are. These stories get built upon over time because the lessons they teach are important for new generations. Folklore can be art, verbal traditions, music, or religion, but they all hold important messages for those who receive them.

These stories highlight the Native American bond with nature.
https://commons.wikimedia.org/wiki/File:Le_G%C3%A9nie_du_Lac_des_Deux-Montagnes.jpg

The following tales include the creation story of the Hopi, the legend of Tigguk from the Inuit tribes, and the Wampanoag tale of Maushop the Giant. These stories highlight the Native American bond with nature so that you get a better understanding of how everything is connected and your responsibility to care for the plants and animals around you.

Through mystical tales of creation and adventure, you get the opportunity to travel the same road that the generations of children traveled before you. Elders of these tribes have repeated these fables for hundreds of years, and now they have reached you so that your imagination can run wild, too.

Creation Myths of Different Tribes

Hopi Tribe Creation Story

Nature is extremely important for indigenous American culture. They understand that without the natural world, people will die, so they honor it. The respect for nature that Indigenous people have is sown into their creation myths. Indigenous people do not see humans as more important than the natural world but rather look at people as part of a complicated spiderweb that connects everything.

The Hopi people understand that the Earth does not belong to humanity; people belong to the Earth. She is the mother of humankind. The Hopi tribe forms part of a larger group called the Pueblo, who come from parts of modern Arizona and New Mexico. The Hopi story of creation is one of the most interesting creation stories in the world.

At the beginning of time, before anything else existed, there were two great beings whose power had no limits. One of these beings was the Spider Woman. She has even more powers than the web-slinger, who wears red and blue tights. The Spider Woman is the Goddess of Earth and is the caregiver of all people on the globe. The other mighty being who was there at the beginning of time is Tawa, the Sun God, who controls everything in the vast sky you look up to at night. He moves the planets, lights up the stars, and throws the meteors that whizz super-fast through the air.

Tawa and the Spider Woman were lonely after spending millions and millions of years together. They had the bright idea to create more living things so they would no longer have to be alone. Tawa ruled the upper worlds, and Spider-Woman ruled the lower worlds. The Land of Shimmering Waters is between the two worlds, where they created the lovely Earth you call home.

Tawa, the Sun God, and the Spider Woman begin a beautiful dance. They twirl around, leaping through all the worlds and swaying and singing at the top of their lungs, creating a powerful, magical wind that fills every corner of the universe. From this magical wind, all the flowers on Earth spring up. They are very colorful and bright. Every color of the rainbow can be seen in their gorgeous petals, and their green leaves and stems stretch into the sky with gratitude to their creators.

After their song and dance session, Tawa feels tired, so he lays down, looking at all the beautiful flowers they just created. He starts to daydream about all kinds of birds flying through the sky, soaring around the mountaintops, and zipping in between the forest trees. He imagines big and small fish jumping through the rivers and diving in and out of the ocean. He thinks of all the trees, some so small that they scrape your ankles and others so giant that they touch the clouds. He dreams of all the animals on Earth, from the mighty Bison running on the open plains to the rattlesnake that wiggles its warning shaker and even the tiny ants who pinch your back when you lay in the tall grass.

The Spider Woman sees Tawa's daydream, and it impresses her. She is amazed at all the different wonderful creatures that Tawa imagines. She is so impressed that hiding all these incredible beings in a dream is not enough for her. The Spider Woman decides to create all of Tawa's dreams from the clay on the Earth, molding them carefully with her loving hands. To this day, the Hopi people honor Tawa and the Spider Woman, who look after them and give them everything they need from the natural world they created. They are like a cosmic mother and father looking after all the people on the planet.

Legendary Heroes: Create Your Own Legend

The Story of Tiggak

Native Americans (or indigenous people) do not all come from one tribe. They have thousands of different traditions, languages, and stories. The Inuit tribes come from the cold parts of America, like Canada and Alaska, where the icy winds bite your skin. Rubbing their hands around a blazing campfire, wrapped in thick furs as the wind whistles through the night, the Elders tell the story of the brave Tiggak.

Long ago, in ancient times, there was a brave and humble man named Tiggak. Food was running low in his village, but because a vicious storm was approaching, many of the hunters were afraid to venture out. As their desperation grew, Tiggak and his son took on the impossible task of going into the rough seas to fish. The strong winds and snow formed ice crystals on their hair while their fingers went numb from tightly clutching their spears.

They got into their skin-covered boat, known as a umiak. The waters grew rougher as waves the size of skyscrapers bashed their small umiak up, down, left, and right. Unfortunately, Tiggak's beloved son passed away in the chaos, so he was forced to carry his body back to the shore. As his eyes welled up with tears and his heart shattered into a hundred pieces, Tiggak buried his son and piled stones on top of his grave.

The skin-covered boat is called an Umiak.

Tiggak could not stand to be separated from his son, so he never returned to the village, choosing instead to construct a home next to where he buried his son. As his grief finally put him to sleep, Tiggak heard rustling outside of his igloo. He woke up, grabbing his spear and carefully approaching the potential danger. He found a fox, a hare, a walrus, and an ice bear digging up his son's grave.

In a heated rage, Tiggak yelled out and, with his mighty strength, attacked the animals, disturbing his son's grave. They tried to fight back but were no match for his incredible power. As he pinned the animals down with his spear, they begged him to spare their lives, explaining why they were doing what they did.

The fox pleaded with Tiggak, saying, "I'm only doing this because I need to get my teeth." The walrus explained, "The only way I can get my whiskers is from your son." The hare explained, "All the internal organs that keep me alive I will get from your son." The ice bear completed their explanation by telling Tiggak, "The only way we can stay alive is by stealing from the dead." Tiggak calmed down because he finally understood that the animals did not take these actions out of cruelty but because they needed to. They taught Tiggak a lesson about the balance of nature and the cycles of life and death. Tiggak let them go, and they repaid his kindness by making sure that his village never went hungry again by always providing them with bountiful hunts.

Maushop the Giant

The Wampanoag people live on the southeastern coast of Massachusetts. Their name in English means "The First People of the Light." Much like many other Native American cultures, the Wampanoag people had a strong connection to the natural world and their surroundings because it was so deeply tied to their daily lives. The Wampanoag people understood that everything is connected. Humanity is part of a complicated and sensitive system, so you must respect nature. The Wampanoag people understood that they could not only selfishly take from nature, but they had to give back because they are part of the Circle of Life and have a duty to look after the plants, animals, rivers, and seas. The story of Maushop the Giant explains how the Wampanoag people learned about their role in the natural cycles of the world.

One day, long ago, the Wampanoag people came across a strong and friendly giant named Maushop, who lived alongside many other magical beings. One of the magical creatures who was Maushop's best friend was a giant frog that could leap as high as the tallest mountain. Maushop was so powerful, and his muscles were so big that when he moved his arms, his clothes would often burst around his bulging biceps. The Wampanoag people loved Maushop because although he was so big and strong, he was gentle and would never harm anybody.

Maushop lived a life of excitement and adventure. He would swim in Popponesset Bay on hot summer days, swinging his windmill arm as he splashed in the cold water. At night, he would make humungous fires on the beach that could be seen from 1,000 miles away! Maushop used these fires to cook whales and other sea creatures because his huge body gave him a massive appetite. Maushop's amazing life made the Wampanoag people love him even more, so they became great friends.

Maushop began helping the Wampanoag with their daily chores.

Maushop began helping the Wampanoag with their daily chores. When they needed fire, he would carry large bundles of heavy wood on his back, and when they were hungry, he would dive deep into the ocean to herd whales onto the shore for them. Maushop started doing so much for the people that they became lazy, just sitting around all day relaxing and doing nothing.

Kehtean the Great Spirit saw this and was unhappy with how the humans had started behaving. The Great Spirit knew that everyone needed to do their part for the Circle of Life to be strong and unbreakable. With a bellowing voice, he called out to Maushop, who got up and ran to him immediately. Kehtean explained that although

Maushop loved the people, he needed to stop doing everything for them because their laziness was going to cause trouble for all living beings in the Circle of Life. When one part of the Circle is out of balance, it can cause everything to collapse, which will lead to catastrophe throughout the land.

Maushop understood what the Great Spirit said, so he decided to leave the people he loved so much. He dove into the ocean, waving goodbye to the Wampanoag and the magical friends he was leaving behind as he went on to greater adventures. When he got far into the ocean, almost out of sight to everybody standing on the sandy shore, the Great Spirit turned him into a giant white whale to spend his days exploring the vast ocean.

Maushop dove into the ocean and spent many days exploring it.
Internet Archive Book Images, No restrictions, via Wikimedia Commons.

Maushop's best friend, the giant frog, would miss his buddy with whom he spent so much time going on all sorts of adventures. He wailed with sorrow, shaking with sadness as he saw his friend swim out into the distance. Kehtean felt sorry for the giant frog who was crying endless tears. He transformed the frog into a huge stone set on top of Gay Head Cliff. Whenever the Womaponoag people look at this stone, they are reminded of how much the Great Spirit cares for them.

The Wampanoag people learned how to get their chores done.

Now that Maushop was gone, the Wampanoag people began scratching their heads, unsure of what to do next because the giant had been doing everything for them for so long. Eventually, they began working together and figuring it out. They learned to work with the water, sea creatures, plants, and animals to meet all of their needs. This is how the Wampanoag people got back in line with the Circle of Life, taking their place as the ones who care for nature and honoring it with their prayers, rituals, and respectful activities.

Create Your Own Legend

1. What lessons have you learned from the legends of Tiggak, Maushop the Giant, Tawa, and the Spider Woman?

_____

_____

_____

_____

_____

_____

_____

_____

_____

2. Which outdoor location in nature is your favorite? Is it the park, the beach, the forest, or somewhere else?

_____

_____

_____

_____

_____

_____

_____

_____

_____

3. Write a story about a legend that you create. Set the story in your favorite place where you spend time in nature.

_____

_____

_____

_____

_____

_____

_____

_____

_____

4. Use a notebook or a piece of paper to draw your legend going on an adventure.
5. Remember that the adventure should teach people an important lesson you want them to learn - like bravery, patience, kindness, love, or caring for nature.

Chapter 2: Native Courage and Leadership

Native American history is riddled with stories woven by the threads of courage, sacrifice, and triumph. It's common knowledge how the Indigenous Americans suffered at the hands of the settlers who hailed from other lands; however, this fact does not take away from the victories they secured in an attempt to protect their land and heritage. Their tales are full to the brim with leaders who defied the odds and faced off against an enemy that surpassed them in weaponry and tactical warfare to preserve their culture.

Their tales are full to the brim with leaders who defied the odds and faced off against an enemy.
https://pixabay.com/illustrations/painting-art-artwork-karl-bodmer-1023111/

In this chapter, you'll find yourself encapsulated with the tales of two of the most famous leaders known in the history of the American Natives: leaders who carved their impact in the young minds of the generations that followed them.

Chief Sitting Bull, the Renowned Leader of the Hunkpapa Lakota Sioux

Sitting Bull. The spiritual and military leader of the Sioux warriors.
https://commons.wikimedia.org/wiki/File:Chief_Sitting_Bull.jpg

The spiritual and military leader of the Sioux warriors is well known for his infamous victory against General George Armstrong Custer at the Battle of Little Bighorn. His fame traveled even further after being involved in the popular Wild West Show with Bill Cody. However, there is more to his story than being a victorious leader and a so-so celebrity. So, who is Sitting Bull?

Life and Background

The Hunkpapa Lakota leader was born in 1831 in the land now commonly known as South Dakota, near the Grand River. When he was born, his father, the chief, named him "Jumping Badger." At a young age, he seemed slightly challenged when it came to his fighting skills and didn't show much promise when it came to waging wars. He was, therefore, called "Slow" -a temporary name for his calm and deliberate attitude until he could prove himself worthy of a better name.

It didn't take long before the young warrior managed to shake off the title given to him earlier. At the young age of 10, he managed to kill his first buffalo, and when he was only 14 years old, he was involved in a fight with rival Crow Indians. During the fight, *Slow* managed to hit one of the enemy warriors with a coup stick, a maneuver called the "count coup." As a result, he was awarded an eagle feather that he wore proudly on his head and was renamed "Tantanka Yotanka," which translates to Sitting Bull or Buffalo Bull who sits down.

At that time, the young man had already proved he possessed all four Lakota virtues: wisdom, bravery, generosity, and fortitude.

Afterward, he joined the Silent Eaters, the Kit Fox Warrior Society, and Strong Heart societies, all of which have the tribe's wellbeing as their main priority. He assisted in expanding the Sioux's hunting grounds into the western territories previously owned and inhabited by the Crow, Shoshone, Assiniboine, and others.

Sitting Bull served as the leader of the entire Lakota Sioux nation, a position never held by any before him, and he was quite vocal with his opinions to avoid all manners of engagement with the white man when others seemed eager to do otherwise. He famously stated, "I have seen nothing that the white man has... which is as good as our right to roam and live on the open plains as we choose."

The fierce leader earned spiritual prominence during his time as the leader of the Lakotas. He often received visions from Wakan-Tanka, "the Everywhere Spirit," where many followers claimed they *DID* come true. Not long after, he officially added "spiritual leader" to the many other titles he had earned.

The Battle of Little Bighorn

The Battle of Little Bighorn.
https://commons.wikimedia.org/wiki/File:Battle_of_the_Little_Big_Horn.jpg

Sitting Bull was no stranger to skirmishes with the U.S. government. In June of 1863, he faced off against the U.S. Army after federal agents withheld food from the Sioux that resided in the reservations as payback for the Minnesota Uprising.

He fought them again in July of 1864 when General Alfred Sully laid siege and surrounded one of the Indian trading villages in the battle of Killdeer Mountain.

These confrontations did nothing but cement Sitting Bull's resolve to not sign any peace treaties with the white man who aimed to eventually relocate his people to a reservation.

These ideals were not unanimous among all Indian leaders, though. In 1868, Red Cloud, chief of the Oglala Teton Dakota Sioux, along with 24 other leaders, went on to sign the Fort Laramie Treaty with Lieutenant General William Tecumseh Sherman. The agreement declared the foundation of the Great Sioux Reservation, along with granting them additional land in Nebraska, Wyoming, and South Dakota.

Sitting Bull's dislike for the treaty earned him much favor among his followers, providing him with more allies (friends) from the Cheyenne and Arapaho tribes.

It didn't take long before he was proven right in his convictions. In 1874, gold was discovered in a sacred site of the Sioux in the Black Hills, which lay within the borders agreed upon for the newly-founded reservation. Needless to say, all peace agreements went out the window once the white man caught wind of the news of the unearthed fortunes.

Many white settlers started falsely claiming the land as their own, while the U.S. government didn't shy away from supporting their illegal claims. They declared new borders in June of 1876 and started threatening the Sioux, who refused to leave.

Among those expected to relocate were members of Sitting Bull's village, who were asked to leave their homes and travel 240 miles in the unforgiving cold.

Holding his stance and refusing to move from his ancestral land, Sitting Bull started preparations for a showdown with the U.S. government. In June 1876, he scored a victory against General George Crook with a group that included Arapaho, Sioux, and Cheyenne. He then moved his army to the Valley of Little Bighorn, where his infamous battle took place.

While camping in Little Bighorn, Sitting Bull took part in the Ceremonial Sun Dance, where he reportedly danced for 36 hours straight and made 50 sacrificial cuts on his arms right before descending into a spiritual trance. During his trance, he observed a vision where he saw U.S. soldiers descending from the sky like grasshoppers. He believed this was a sign of an upcoming victory over their oppressors.

He was not wrong. On the 25th of June, General George Custer led around 300 men (the numbers vary from one account to another) into the Valley, where he was met with 3,000 strong native men on the battlefield. Sitting Bull, being older than the normal fighting age, ensured the safety of the women and children while handing over the army's leadership to Crazy Horse. His two nephews, White Bull and One Bull, took part in the battle, protected by their uncle's medicine. The Sioux men fought bravely, taking out the entire force of General Custer's army in a swift victory, later known as *Custer's Last Stand.*

The Aftermath

As a result of the victory, the U.S. government felt scorned and humiliated that they doubled down on their pursuits of the Sioux men. The white settlers started targeting the livelihood of the Sioux by killing the buffalo herds they depended on to survive.

In return, Sitting Bull wisely decided to protect his flock by leading them to Canada in May of 1877. However, with little food to go around, the chief was forced to make a deal with the U.S. Army, where he surrendered himself in exchange for the absolution of his people. As a result of his sacrifice, he was taken prisoner at South Dakota's Fort Randall for two years, and then he was sent to the Standing Rock Reservation.

Wilma Mankiller: The First Female Principal Chief of the Cherokee Nation

Wilma Mankiller is famous for being the first indigenous female chief of the Cherokee nation.
https://commons.wikimedia.org/wiki/File:Wilma_Mankiller_1998.jpg

Wilma Mankiller is a modern-day inspiration and hero to a lot of youth in the current century, both of native descent and otherwise. Wilma is famous for being the first indigenous female chief of the Cherokee nation. She was the first woman to be elected to ascend the position of chief in one of the prime native tribes. She may seem familiar if you're used to carrying change in your pocket; she was honored alongside other female pioneers by appearing on a series of quarters!. She spent the better part of her life fighting for the rights of Indigenous Americans.

Early Life

Mankiller was born in Tahlequah, Oklahoma, the nation's capital, on November 18, 1945. She had ten siblings who shared the same name, which translated in Cherokee culture to something akin to Captain or Major. The name referenced the position of a person who watched over the Cherokee population and their villages.

Growing up, Wilma lived in a simple household with no electricity, plumbing, or any means of communication, such as a telephone.

Wilma was moved with her family, ages 10 and 11, as part of the Bureau of Indian Affairs' relocation strategy to a low-income San Francisco neighborhood. She often described this move as her very own little trail of tears about the relocation of her Cherokee ancestors from Tennessee over the Trail of Tears in the 1830s.

The government passed several laws, including the one relocating the aboriginal tribes, intending to sell their reservation lands and break up their settlements. The bills were passed under the pretense of luring the natives to the bigger cities with the promise of better opportunities and jobs when, in fact, it was an effort to assimilate them into the American culture and erase their own.

These bills also resulted in the termination of over 100 tribes and the removal of around 1.3 million acres of native lands. They made sure to shut down health facilities and certain schools in the reservations. Most natives who made the move suffered from poverty and horrible living conditions, finding it extremely hard to get used to life in the city.

Mankiller's Activism

Wilma participated in her first bold act of activism in 1969. She participated in the American Indian Movement's demonstration at Alcatraz, where they claimed a "right of discovery" over the federal prison located in San Francisco Bay. This occupation lasted for 18 months. Reversing the termination measures and reestablishing the cultural institutions and schools on the American Native Island constituted the sum total of the demands.

The American Indian Movement's Flag.
Tripodero, CC0, via Wikimedia Commons:
https://commons.wikimedia.org/wiki/File:Flag_of_the_American_Indian_Movement_V2.svg

She made it her mission to instill power and pride back in the Native communities. She became a director at the Native American Youth Center in California, aiming to support and protect the native youth from life on the streets.

Mankiller assisted the indigenous by teaching them about the ins and outs of protecting and exercising treaty rights and tribal sovereignty during the court dispute between Pacific Gas and Electric and the Pit River Tribe. This knowledge traveled back with her when she returned to her Cherokee home.

Mankiller had become a divorced single mother of two girls by 1977, living in her native Oklahoma by a creek in her automobile.

She was eager to work and was successful in landing a position as the economic stimulus coordinator for the Cherokee Nation. This position made her creation of the Cherokee Nation's Community Development Department possible.

Her foundation focused primarily on improving living conditions and supporting the Cherokee nation. Her first project was in Bell, Oklahoma, where 200 native people were living in poverty and without access to water. Empowering the people to work together, and with her ability to organize the workforce and secure enough funding, they succeeded in erecting a 16-mile-long waterline in just 14 months. This feat inspired the movie "The Cherokee Word for Water."

Achievements and Recognition

Wilma became the first female Principal Chief of the Cherokee Nation when she assumed that role in 1985. She served in her role for 10 years, taking care of 140,000 members and being in charge of a budget that amounted to 75 million dollars, which reached 150 million dollars by the end of her time as their leader. During her tenure, tribal enrollment doubled from 68,000 to 170,000. As the tribe chief, she served as the custodian of centuries-long Cherokee traditions and legal codes.

She later established a center for drug misuse prevention and opened three rural healthcare clinics.

She was involved in establishing the U.S. Department of Justice's Office of Tribal Justice. During her leadership, infant mortality significantly declined, while educational accomplishments were on the rise in the Cherokee community.

In 1987, she received the Woman of the Year award from MS Magazine.

She was honored for her efforts to uplift and support her home community by being inducted into the National Women's Hall of Fame in 1993 and by receiving the Presidential Medal of Freedom, the nation's highest civilian honor, from President Bill Clinton in 1998. "Mankiller: A Chief and Her People," her autobiography, was released in 2000.

Wilma Mankiller lost her battle with pancreatic cancer at the age of 64 on April 6th, 2010. She left behind a legacy of strength and resilience for the native youth that came after her.

Test of Knowledge

1. What was Chief Sitting Bull's Birth name, and how did he earn the name Sitting Bull?
2. Who led the charge in the Battle of Little Bighorn?
3. What was the name of the U.S. General that Sitting Bull fought in the battle of Killdeer Mountain?
4. Where was Wilma Mankiller Born?
5. Why was Mankiller's family relocated to San Francisco?
6. When did Mankiller move back to Oklahoma?

Chapter 3: Tales of the Earth and Sky

People have been looking up at the stars for thousands and maybe millions of years. Try to count the stars in the sky. You'll see that it seems like they go on forever. The endless stars in the sky remind humanity how small people are compared to the universe. From the beginning of time, humankind has looked up to the sky to tell stories. The stars, moon, sun, and planets have whispered stories that are kept alive to infinity, and the indigenous people of America have kept many of the tales that the universe has told.

People have been looking up at the stars for thousands and maybe millions of years.
Mathias Krumbholz, CC BY-SA 3.0 <https://creativecommons.org/licenses/by-sa/3.0>, via Wikimedia Commons: https://commons.wikimedia.org/wiki/File:Stars_01_(MK).jpg

The Great Bear and the Seven Birds

This story is all about the Big Dipper and the constellation that the ancient Romans and Greeks called Corona Borealis. In America, these patterns in the sky are called different names. The Opaskwayak Cree Nation called the Big Dipper "Mista Muskwa," which is the Great Bear. They called the Corona Borealis "Tepahkoop Pinesisuk," or the Seven Birds.

The tale of how the Great Bear and the Seven Birds flew up into the heavens is ancient. Long ago, there were giant bears that roamed the face of the planet. The ground would shake, and dust would fill the air with the force of their huge paws hitting the ground with a thunderous "BOOM!"

The giant bears were so big and strong that every other living thing on earth was terrified of them. The bears used their incredible power to bully everyone to get what they wanted. The leader of these wicked bears was the Great Bear. Whenever he entered a new village, he wanted offerings from the people living there. He went so crazy with power that he eventually stopped asking for offerings, taking whatever his huge arms could carry.

The Great Bear had no love or care in his heart for other living beings.
https://pixabay.com/illustrations/ai-generated-bear-animal-wild-8666173/

The Great Bear had no love or care in his heart for other living beings. He would ravage a village, crushing anyone who tried to stop him. Sometimes, he ate a village's whole winter supply so they would starve and struggle during the cold months. After years of getting bullied by the Great Bear, a group of elders from several villages came together so that they could figure out how to stop him.

The village leaders choose from among them seven of the best hunters and trackers. These happened to be the Seven Birds, who were highly skilled at following any beast for thousands of miles. Although the Great Bear was bigger, the Seven Birds were great at working as a team, which is why they were such brilliant hunters.

The Great Bear had his own team of birds who loyally served him for decades. These birds were the Crow, the Raven, and the Magpie. They were scavengers, so they followed the Great Bear around, eating all his leftovers. The Crow, Raven, and Magpie warned the Great Bear of the Seven Birds, who were speeding directly to his den to attack him one morning.

The cowardly bully fled when he heard that the Seven Birds coming for him. They chased him around the Earth four times as his gigantic paws splashed through the salty ocean waves, stumbled through the widest deserts, and climbed over the tallest mountains. In the fourth round, they were moving faster than a rocket, so they zoomed up into the air. The Great Bear's lungs began to burn, and his heart pounded in his chest as he grew more and more tired. Eventually, he got so tired that he turned around to face the skilled hunting birds.

The Robin, or as the Opaskwayak Cree call him, the Pipiciw, who was the bravest of the Seven Birds, dove in beak first, cutting open the Great Bear. The Bear let out a roar and shook with pain, shaking his blood onto all the leaves of the trees, which is why they change color in the fall. A drop of blood fell onto the Robin, which is why all robins today have a red chest.

The Creator of the universe was looking down and watching the chase and fight from the heavens. To honor Robin's bloodline, the Creator gave them speckled eggs that looked like the night sky to remind people of this amazing day when the Great Bear was defeated by tiny birds. He then placed the Seven Birds and the Great Bear in the sky to remind people of all generations of the courage of the Seven Birds. Today, the Great Bear is the Big Dipper constellation, and the Seven Birds are the

Corona Borealis constellation.

Today, the Great Bear is the Big Dipper constellation.
Stellarium map with additions by Bob King; source: Robert Benjamin., CC BY-SA 3.0
<https://creativecommons.org/licenses/by-sa/3.0>, via Wikimedia Commons:
https://commons.wikimedia.org/wiki/File:Arc-Big-Dipper-map_S2.jpg

The Lost Children

For hundreds of generations, the Black Foot culture has been telling the story of the lost children. This tale is about what happens when people are not kind to the children they have been gifted by the Great Spirit.

A long time ago, close to the beginning of the Earth, six brothers had no parents. The orphan boys did not have a home and would wander from place to place every night, finding a new spot to lay their heads. The cracked lips of their dry mouths stuck together as their stomachs consistently cried out for food. They had no family, so they scavenged the little they had, wearing the ripped clothes that traveling hunters discarded to lighten their loads.

They played and cuddled with the village dogs. The dogs and the boys grew to become great friends and always helped one another in their difficult world. The brothers often shared their beds with the dogs to keep warm on windy nights when the cool breeze ripped through their tattered clothing.

No one in the village treated the children with kindness. The other kids would throw stones at them and chase them with sticks. They made fun of their broken clothing and cackled at their long, matted hair. Once a year, when summer started, the village would open the hunting season by tracking buffalo herds. They would gift the children of the village yellow calf hides to celebrate their success, but they always turned a cold shoulder on the six brothers, giving them nothing.

So tired from how cruelly the village people had treated them all those years, the brothers began fantasizing about a better life.
https://commons.wikimedia.org/wiki/File:Ernest_Smith_Sky_Woman_1936.jpg

So tired from how cruelly the village people had treated them all those years, the brothers began fantasizing about a better life. They were determined to leave the village, and because people had treated them so horribly, they no longer wanted to be human. They began arguing about what they should transform into.

One brother shouted out, "We should be flowers so that we can be beautiful and everyone will admire our gorgeous colors."

The other brothers answered, "If we are flowers, all the buffaloes will eat us."

"Maybe we can be stones. They are strong, and no one can harm them," another brother suggested. "People and animals will trample on us because big rocks break into smaller stones," one of the brothers answered.

"We can be water and flow as far as the land can take us," said one of the brothers. "But then, all the animals and people will drink us," another responded.

Finally, the most intelligent of the boys came up with the perfect solution. They could be stars because they'll be high up in the sky, away from the harsh villagers. Everyone would look at them to tell the change of seasons and admire their beauty. Stars remain forever, so they will always have a place to stay in the sky.

One brother blew on a feather that floated them high up into the sky. He warned everyone to close their eyes and never look back. One of the brothers stubbornly disobeyed and looked down at the village for one last time. He was transformed into the Smoking Star comet.

The boy was transformed into the Smoking Star comet.
https://pixabay.com/illustrations/space-stars-comet-astronomy-1486556/

The boys floated high into the upper world, landing on a lush green prairie filled with all kinds of aromatic plant life. They approached the huge teepee where Sun Man and his wife, Moon Woman, lived. Sun Man asked the boys why they had traveled so far from Earth. They told him about how unkind the village people were to them. Moon Woman wept with soul-wrenching sadness. She called them the Lost Children.

Sun Man was enraged by the people's hardened hearts. He shone brightly on them, drying up all the water and turning the world into a desert where nothing could grow. All the plants, animals, and people were hungry and thirsty as they breathed in nothing but dust. The dogs that had befriended the boys in the village howled, crying out at Moon Woman and Sun Man to show them mercy.

Sun Man saw the suffering of all the animals and felt sorry for them because he only meant to punish the unkind humans. He sent them rain that brought back all the plants, trees, and rivers for the animals and people to enjoy. The Lost Children are now the Pleiades stars bunched up together in the sky far from the village, reminding people to always be kind to children. They are surrounded by many smaller stars, which are the dogs who found their way back to their lost human friends.

Raven Steals the Light

This story of the cunning trickster, Raven, comes from the Haida people. In the early days of the Earth, there lived a powerful chief who loved his daughter more than anything on the planet. He always got her gifts to show how much he cared for her. One day, the chief took the sun and moon out of the sky and into his large teepee as a gift for his daughter. She leaped with excitement, thanking her beloved father for this incredible present.

Due to the sun and moon now being shielded in the chief's private home, the entire world was pitch black and covered in a blanket of darkness. Nobody could hunt or fish because it was too difficult to see. They either stumbled around, tripping over everything, or crawled on their hands and knees to feel the ground.

The Raven was the most intelligent of all the birds.

The Raven was the most intelligent of all the birds. He said that he would go get the moon and sun back from the chief. The Raven tried to charm the chief with his fancy words, but the stubborn leader would not give him the sun or the moon because it made his daughter so happy. The Raven knew he would need to come up with a plan.

One night, when the chief's daughter went to the river to drink some water, the Raven shape-shifted into a tiny fish and dove into her cup. The daughter never noticed the small fish and swallowed him whole. The Raven began to grow in her belly, transforming into a baby, and the daughter gave birth to a boy named Raven. As Raven grew, he asked his grandfather for the sun and the moon, which the loving chief openly gave to his grandson. Raven returned the sun and the moon to the sky so the people could now once again hunt under the moonlight and sunlight.

Shoot for the Stars Quiz

Write down the letter with the right answer to each question. The answers are at the bottom of the quiz. Do not peak before you complete the quiz. When you are finished, check your answers to see how well you've done.

1. **What is the moral of the story of the Great Bear and the Seven Birds?**
   a. If you work as a team, you can take down big challenges.
   b. A and C.
   c. You should never use your power to bully others.
   d. If you train hard, you will be able to run fast.

2. **What is the Great Bear's Name in the Opaskwayak Cree language?**
   a. Tepahkoop Pinesisuk.
   b. Tigguk.
   c. Flower.
   d. Mista Muskwa.

3. **The Corona Borealis constellation is also known by which name in the Opaskwayak Cree Nation?**
   a. The Big Dipper.
   b. Tepahkoop Pinesisuk.
   c. Mista Muskwa.
   d. The Small Dipper.

4. **Why did the six brothers run away from the village in the story of The Lost Children?**
   a. The village people were unkind to them.
   b. They didn't like the taste of buffalo.
   c. The camp dogs were always biting them.
   d. They wanted to see how fast they could run.

5. **What did the Sun Man do to punish the humans in the story of The Lost Children?**
   a. He flooded the village.
   b. He did nothing.
   c. He caused a drought and dried out the world, so the people were hungry and thirsty.
   d. He made mosquitoes bite the people while they slept.

6. How big was the new home that the Lost Children slept in with Sun Man and Moon Woman, his wife?

  a. The size of the Grand Canyon.

  b. As big as the sky.

  c. Tall like a skyscraper.

  d. As big as a celebrity mansion.

7. Which Indigenous Nation does the story of The Lost Children come from?

  a. Cheyenne.

  b. Apache.

  c. Cherokee.

  d. Black Foot.

8. In the story "Raven Steals the Light," what happened to the people when the chief first put the sun and the moon in his home?

  a. It got so dark nobody could hunt or fish.

  b. Schoolchildren could not study.

  c. It got cold outside.

  d. Everyone was afraid of the dark.

9. What skill did the Raven use to get back the sun and moon?

  a. Strength and bravery.

  b. Intelligence and cunning.

  c. Love and care.

  d. Beauty.

10. Which indigenous nation does the story of "Raven Steals the Light" come from?

  a. The Haida.

  b. Black Foot.

  c. The Pueblo.

  d. The Aztecs.

Chapter 4: Spirit of the Buffalo: Stories of Community

The Native Americans always knew how important it was to respect other living beings. Their stories speak about how, in nature, everyone and everything is connected and depends on each other. This chapter brings you two tales about the creature the Native Americans have a powerful connection to — the buffalo.

Their stories speak about how, in nature, everyone and everything is connected and depends on each other.

https://pixabay.com/illustrations/ai-generated-shaman-mystical-forest-8671770/

The first story is about a beautiful young woman sent as a messenger to teach the Lakota how to live peacefully and happily together. The second tale shows how the Plains tribes explain the origin of the buffalo hunt — the activity that helped them survive and build strong communities.

The Lakota Legend of the White Buffalo Calf Woman

A few American Indian tribes considered the buffalo a priceless gift from their creator. This is confirmed by several stories, but none is as fascinating as the White Buffalo Calf Woman Lakota Legend.

The story begins with two young Lakota men who were given a very important task. They were asked to seek out the buffalos because the tribe didn't know where these animals lived.

So, the two young men were sent to explore the land on horseback. They couldn't have been riding an hour when they saw something approaching them from a great distance. They could see what it was, and because they thought that it might be a buffalo or another dangerous animal, they jumped into the nearby bushes to hide.

The two men realized that the figure approaching them was a beautiful woman.
https://pixabay.com/illustrations/ai-generated-woman-native-american-8549063/

As they waited in their hiding place, they realized the figure approaching them was a beautiful woman. She carried a bundle of sage in her arms. She also saw them as the bushes weren't thick enough to hide them. The woman stopped in front of the bush and looked at the two young men. They were enhanced by her beauty. One of them even said that he would like to marry the woman because she was the most beautiful one he had ever seen in his life. However, the other one said that the woman's beauty means she is holy and above ordinary people.

The woman heard the two men talking as she approached them even closer. When she was right in front of the bush, she put the bundle of sage she was carrying on the ground and beckoned the young men to come to her. She asked them what they wished for.

The man who said that he wanted to marry the woman immediately went to her and put his arms on hers, claiming her. Suddenly, the sky grew darker, and the wind picked up, creating a whirlwind and dust cloud, making the man and the woman disappear. Then, the wind quieted down, the dust settled, and the woman was standing where she was before. She was holding her sage bundle in her arms again, but the man disappeared. In his place, only a pile of bones was on the ground.

The other man wasn't frightened but stood in awe of this woman's power. Then, the woman told him she was going to visit his tribe. She urged Bull Walking Upright, a young Lakota guy, to return to his tribe and inform the others that she was on her way because she wanted to meet him.

She also instructed him to ask the other people to gather up and reposition their tents in a circle.

Additionally, they had to leave a gap in the circle pointing north. The woman concluded by saying that she intended to meet Bull Walking Upright at the largest tipi located in the circle's middle.

The young man hurried home and immediately recounted what the beautiful woman ordered. The others followed the directions and awaited her arrival. When the woman reached their camp, she had the sage bundle with her. Stepping into the circle, she revealed that she was hiding something under the bundle. She had brought a small pipe made of a vivid red stone as a present for the tribe. It has a buffalo's outline on it.

Bull Walking Upright was given the pipe by the woman, who also promised to teach him the proper prayers to offer to the Creator.

She told him that whenever he prays to the Creator for help, he must use the tiny pipe in the ceremony.

The woman also revealed that the pipe had a magical ability. When the tribe was hungry, they should lay out the pipe in the air, and it would summon the buffalos near their territory. This way, the hunters can provide food for their families.

The pipe would summon the buffalos near their territory.
Evan Howard, CC BY-SA 2.0 <https://creativecommons.org/licenses/by-sa/2.0>, via Wikimedia Commons: https://commons.wikimedia.org/wiki/File:Bison_Hunt_(2417618531.5).jpg

The woman had another lesson to teach the people. She explained to Bull Walking Upright that the earth that people live on is their mother. In order for everyone to live and use the Earth together peacefully, they need to respect Mother Earth and each other.

In addition, the woman instructed the tribe to dress like Mother Earth for ceremonies and taught them prayers they could recite to her.

They ought to dress in the hues that they can observe in nature, which are white, brown, red, and black. Furthermore, they would quickly discover that these hues match those of the buffalo.

Lastly, the beautiful woman reminded the tribe to always smoke the pipe before ceremonies and before creating a treaty. She said it would help bring peace because smoking the pipe would make everyone more peaceful. With a calmer mind, they could make better decisions and focus on asking for blessings from the Creator and Mother Nature. If they ask for something with the help of the pipe, they'll be sure to receive it.

After saying the last words, the beautiful woman turned, and stepping out of the circle, she slowly started to walk away while the tribe watched her in awe, their eyes shining with gratitude. She suddenly stopped and lay down on the ground. As she stood up, she transformed into a black buffalo cow. She rose like a red buffalo cow and lay down again. She changed into a brown buffalo cow when she lay down for the third time and into a white buffalo cow when she lay down for the fourth time.

The white buffalo then walked away from the people, disappearing over the hills in the north.

From this day on, Bull Walking Upright followed her directions. He kept the tiny red pipe with him wrapped up, only unwrapping it when it was time to gather the tribe and begin a ceremony. Before each lesson, he said the prayers the woman taught him.

Eventually, Bull Walking Upright grew old and too weak to hold ceremonies. He was over 100 years old and knew it was time to give the duty to another tribe member. He chose Sunrise — a wise man who was happy to learn the prayers and take the pipe. When it was time for him to step down, he again passed the pipe and the lessons to a worthy young tribe member, and so they have traveled down from many generations ever since. And, just as the woman promised, the pipe brought happiness and peace to the tribe.

Do you think the pipe made their community stronger? If so, how? What made this gift so powerful?

Have you ever received or given a gift that helped you become closer to someone?

The Story of How the Buffalo Hunt Began

The Plain Tribes were always known for their tight-knit community.
https://commons.wikimedia.org/wiki/File:Native_Americans_from_Southeastern_Idaho_-_NARA_-_519243.tif

The Plain Tribes were always known for their tight-knit community. In these warm communities, children did their chores obediently, the adults watched over them, and everyone looked out for each other.

Some were hunters and farmers, others warriors, and some did a little bit of everything. Some tribes moved around during the summer and winter but had a home to return to in the spring when they planted their crops and again in the fall when the crops were ready to harvest.

One of the activities that forged the Plain Tribe communities was hunting. They particularly liked hunting buffalos — and had lots of interesting ways to catch these large and powerful animals. For example, sometimes, they would chase them until the animal had to stop out of exhaustion. Others would pretend to be young buffalo crying desperately for help in order to lure an adult away from its herd.

Most tribes used the different parts of the buffalo for food, clothes, and other household items, once again involving the entire community in making these products.

However, according to their legends, the tribes didn't always hunt buffalo. The story of how the hunt for this magnificent animal began is a unique tale of community.

A long time ago, it wasn't the people who hunted the buffalo but the other way around. Buffalos — with the power of 20 bulls and a surprising speed of over 30 miles per hour — are moody creatures. They would attack and eat people if they were in a dark mood.

To keep the peace between people and buffalos, two birds — the hawk and the magpie — did their best to keep the animals away from people. However, this wasn't enough. Ultimately, they decided that all animals and people would enter a race, and the winners of this race could eat the losers!

Of course, the big and confident buffalos were happy to race, even though they knew that the course was a long trail around a dangerous mountain. Neika, the bravest of the buffalos, entered the race first.

The people were more cautious because they knew that they would get tired much faster. However, they had a plan for preventing fatigue from wearing them down and giving up before the finish line. After all, the stakes were high, and they risked being eaten by the buffalos and other scary animals. So, they set on to find a secret medicine that would make them strong enough to beat everyone else and reach the finish line first.

Meanwhile, all the other animals were preparing for the race, too. Some did this by painting themselves in vibrant colors. The magpie turned its tail, shoulders, and head white, and all the plain-looking animals maintained their bright coloring.

When everyone was ready, they lined up at the start line. Someone gave the signal, and the race was on. As they ran, Neika took the lead, with the magpie, the hawk, and the people behind her. The rest, like the slithering snakes, playful rabbits, buzzing insects, the cunning but not-quite-fast enough wolves, the diligent but tiny ants, and the other colorful birds, were following the leaders far behind. Despite their disadvantage, all animals tried encouraging themselves to run faster. The wolves howled, the insects beat their wings more quickly, the birds sang, and so on. It was undoubtedly a fascinating race to watch!

When they approached the mountainside, they picked up so much dust that no one was able to see each other, so they could only focus on themselves. The magpie and the hawk both knew that they could fly faster and catch up with Neika, but they chose to preserve their strengths until they were near the finish line. Then, they simply whooshed by Neika and won the race. As they made their circles of victory above the racecourse, they noticed that many animals had fallen. However, they were happy because they had no intention of eating anyone. They just wanted to help the people and stop the buffalos from hunting them.

When the two birds told the people that they had won the race in their name, they decided to start hunting and eating the buffalos. The buffalos heard this and ordered their young to hide to save them. However, before they allowed the youngsters to scurry away, they told them to take some of the leftover human flesh and put it in front of their chests. The young buffaloes did this and went to hide away as the people began their hunt. They spared the young ones until they grew up and then hunted them, too, using them all except for the bits of flesh in front of their chest. To this day, this part of the buffalo is not used because it's said to come from humans and not from animals.

When the two birds told the people that they had won the race in their name, they decided to start hunting and eating the buffalos.
https://commons.wikimedia.org/wiki/File:Buffalo_Hunt.jpg

The people saw that none of the other animals were against them, so they spared every last one. They welcomed them into their lives, forming one big happy community. They only asked the birds for some of their fallen feathers to use for headpieces and other traditional decorations.

What do you think of the clever way the magpie and the hawk saved the people? And what about the people's decision to spare the other creatures and welcome them into their community?

Do you think it's important to welcome others into your life? Why?

True or False

Read the following sentences carefully. Some are true, others are not. Can you pick which ones are true?

- The Lakota didn't know where the buffalos lived.
- The beautiful woman said that she would bring a gift to the Lakota.
- The woman transformed four times, showing the four colors of the buffalo.
- The Lakota had forgotten about the pipe.
- People and the buffalos always lived in peace.
- The magpie and the hawk were on the side of the people.
- All the animals had vibrant colors on them before the race.
- The people started hunting buffalos after the race.

Chapter 5: Visions of Hope and Future: Prophecies

Many famous prophets have been predicting either a fascinating future or a bleak fate for generations. Like most other cultures and religions, the Native Americans also have prophets who show visions of both hope and doom. Many of their prophecies are centered on the latter, but interestingly, they also provide hope. Learning about them is like diving into a bottomless pit and finding your way back out unharmed.

The Hopi people belong to different tribes in northeastern Arizona, but most identify themselves with the Hopi Tribe of Arizona.

Internet Archive Book Images, No restrictions, via Wikimedia Commons:
https://commons.wikimedia.org/wiki/File:American_Indians_-
_first_families_of_the_Southwest_(1920)_(14589572319).jpg

The Hopi Prophecy

The Hopi people belong to different tribes in northeastern Arizona, but most identify themselves with the Hopi Tribe of Arizona. The Hopi Tribe is a sovereign nation in the United States, meaning it governs itself.

One of the most distinctive aspects of Hopi culture is its kachina religious practices. Spiritual creatures known as kachinas are thought to symbolize many facets of the natural world, spirits, and ancestors.

Hopi ceremonies involving kachinas are performed throughout the year to ensure the community's well-being, promote fertility, and bring rain for the crops to flourish. It is from one of these spiritual beings that the Hopi Prophecy originates.

According to their tradition, the Blue Star Kachina (also known as Saquasohuh) is said to represent the coming of the end of the world or a significant transition period (an apocalypse). Saquasohuh is a powerful spiritual being who will appear as a bright blue star in the sky — a moment that will herald major changes on Earth.

It doesn't refer to the blue stars that already exist in the night sky, like those in the Orion constellation. Many believe that Saquasohuh will be brighter than the brightest of the stars, and a few others say that it will be as huge as a mountain.

The arrival of this star is believed to bring purification and a spiritual awakening. This massive transformation won't necessarily be swift and calm. A few of the Hopi prophecies predict the appearance of the Red Star Kachina soon after Saquasohuh, which will result in destruction, chaos, and the end of the current world. It will be as big and bright as Saquasohuh.

However, just as they herald massive transformations and destruction, true to their Hopi prophecy name, they also give hope. This cleansing of the world can be avoided by maintaining harmony with nature and living under spiritual principles. These principles include:

- **Connection to Nature:** Many Native American spiritual beliefs emphasize a deep connection to the natural world. Nature is considered sacred, and humans are considered a part of, rather than separate from, the environment. Respect for all living beings and the Earth itself forms the foundation of their beliefs.
- **Harmony and Balance:** Balance is an essential concept in their spirituality. This includes finding balance within oneself and

maintaining harmony with others and the natural world. Imbalance is often seen as the root of illness, conflict, and other problems.

They emphasize the interconnectedness of all things.
Southwestern State Teachers College, No restrictions, via Wikimedia Commons:
https://commons.wikimedia.org/wiki/File:%22Buffalo_in_Western_Okla.%22_(Oklahoma)_Nati
ve_American_and_Bison_art_detail,_Oracle,_The_(1921)_(14788226263)_(cropped).jpg

- **Interconnectedness:** They emphasize the interconnectedness of all things. "Things" is the keyword here. It doesn't simply imply the connection between humans but also their connection to the natural world, their ancestors, the spiritual realm, and everything else.

- **Respect for Elders and Ancestors:** Elders hold a special place in many Native American cultures, as they are valued for their wisdom, experience, and connection to tradition. Ancestors are also revered, and their guidance and protection are often sought through rituals and ceremonies, which brings the next point.
- **Ceremonies and Rituals:** Ceremonies and rituals play a significant role in spiritual practices. These may include rituals for healing, prayer, purification, rites of passage, and honoring the cycles of nature. These cycles include scientific ones like nitrogen and water and spiritual ones like birth and death.

Music, dance, and storytelling are the essence of their ceremonies, and they are known to use sacred objects like drums, feathers, and herbs to bring their ceremonies to fruition.

- **Spiritual Guardians and Guides:** They believe in the existence of spiritual guardians, guides, and helpers, but they aren't always immaterial or in the spiritual form. They may take the form of animal spirits, ancestors, or other beings who offer protection and assistance on the peoples' spiritual journey.
- **Respect for Diversity:** Their spiritual traditions recognize and honor the diversity of beliefs and practices among different tribes and individuals. There is no single absolute Native American religion — each tribe has its own unique spiritual teachings and practices.
- **Living in Harmony with Natural Cycles:** They emphasize the importance of living in accordance with the natural cycles of the earth, like the changing seasons and the cycles of the moon. This may involve practices such as planting and harvesting in harmony with the seasons or conducting ceremonies to mark significant celestial events.

In essence, the Hopi prophecy predicts doom but also provides solutions to prevent it from happening. Surprisingly, they are scientifically relevant. Over the years, human negligence of nature has made the threat of global warming a clear and present danger. It has become more than important to work toward environmental stewardship and spiritual renewal, which involves:

Many Native American tribes view the land as sacred and recognize their spiritual connection to it.

- **A Sacred Relationship with the Land:** Many Native American tribes view the land as sacred and recognize their spiritual connection to it. They have a deep sense of responsibility and stewardship toward the environment, as the Earth is seen as a living entity deserving of reverence and protection.

- **Traditional Ecological Knowledge:** Indigenous peoples have accumulated generations of traditional ecological knowledge (TEK) about their local ecosystems, including plant and animal species, seasonal cycles, and sustainable resource management practices. This knowledge is passed down orally through storytelling, ceremonies, and everyday practices.

- **Sustainable Resource Use:** They have been historically practicing sustainable resource use, harvesting only what is necessary and ensuring that resources are replenished for future generations. Traditional hunting, fishing, agriculture, and gathering techniques involve careful observation of ecological patterns and cycles to avoid overexploitation.

- **Conservation Practices:** They have developed numerous conservation practices to preserve biodiversity and maintain healthy ecosystems. These include controlled burning to manage forests, rotating agricultural fields to prevent soil depletion, and creating protected areas for wildlife.
- **Ritual Practices:** Many Native American ceremonies and rituals are dedicated to honoring the Earth and its natural cycles. They involve prayers, offerings, and symbolic gestures to express gratitude for the gifts of the land and to ask for guidance in living harmoniously with nature.
- **Environmental Advocacy:** Indigenous peoples have been at the forefront of environmental advocacy (support) efforts locally and globally. Many tribes have fought to protect their ancestral lands from environmental degradation caused by extractive industries, pollution, and unsustainable development. They are known to advocate for the recognition of land rights and the incorporation of indigenous knowledge into conservation efforts.
- **Community-Based Approaches:** Environmental stewardship is often community-driven, with decision-making processes guided by traditional values, consensus-building, and collective responsibility. This approach lends a strong sense of solidarity and collaboration in protecting the environment for future generations.

This prophecy signifies that nature is a powerful force with the potential to make or break the world. If it's taken care of, it will build a sustainable future for all the living beings on this planet, but if it's misused, it will transform into a force of death and destruction by inviting Saquasohuh (the Blue Star Kachina) into the skies. In short, caring for all natural things is critical for preventing the Hopi prophecy from coming to fruition.

The Seventh Generation Prophecy

It is a fact that Native Americans are at the forefront of battling environment-harming practices.
Frithjof Schuon, CC0, via Wikimedia Commons:
https://commons.wikimedia.org/wiki/File:Detail_from_%E2%80%9CApparition_of_the_Buffalo
_Calf_Maiden%E2%80%9D_(1959)_by_Frithjof_Schuon.jpg

It is a fact that Native Americans are at the forefront of battling environment-harming practices, and this drive primarily arises from the Seventh Generation Prophecy. It is a concept deeply rooted in the spiritual beliefs of many indigenous peoples in the U.S. While it varies among different tribes and nations, the prophecy generally emphasizes the connections between generations and the responsibility of present-day actions to future generations – going about seven generations into the future!

The origins of the Seventh Generation Prophecy can be traced back to various Native American oral traditions and teachings. Among some tribes, it is believed that decisions made by the current generation should be guided by their impact on the well-being of the seventh generation yet to come.

For instance, if a person is about to decide their career, they should consider its impact on seven generations of people after them. If they are considering engineering as their career, they should try to make a difference that would benefit seven generations down the line. The same goes for painting, agriculture, science, and virtually anything else. This concept underscores the importance of sustainability, stewardship of the land, and the preservation of cultural values and traditions.

Key aspects of the Seventh Generation Prophecy include:

- It emphasizes the interconnectedness of all living beings and the recognition that actions taken today have consequences that reverberate through future generations. It reflects a holistic worldview that acknowledges the complex web of relationships between humans, nature, and the spiritual realm.

- It underscores the responsibility of the present generation to act as stewards of the Earth and its resources. This involves making decisions that put future generations' long-term well-being over short-term gains and ensuring the sustainability of natural ecosystems and cultural practices. For example, suppose an engineer can make quick bucks out of a project that will potentially harm the region's future. In that case, they will reject it and make sure that it doesn't become a reality.

- In addition to environmental stewardship, the prophecy often emphasizes the importance of preserving cultural traditions, languages, and knowledge systems. This includes passing down ancestral teachings and wisdom to successive generations and ensuring the continuity of indigenous cultures and identities.

- One of the prime beliefs goes something like this: the Seventh Generation Prophecy is guided by spiritual forces and ancestral wisdom. Ceremonies, prayers, and rituals may be conducted to seek guidance and blessings for the future and to honor the spirits of ancestors who have come before and those who are yet to come. It is more like shaping the future through the wisdom of history.

- It has inspired indigenous communities to advocate for (actively support and push for) social and environmental justice and recognize Native American rights and sovereignty. Activism efforts often center on issues like land rights, environmental conservation, and cultural revitalization, focusing on creating a better world for future generations.

Overall, the Seventh Generation Prophecy is a guiding principle for Native American culture, shaping their worldview, values, and actions about the past, present, and future. It highlights the importance of living in harmony with the Earth and each other and the deep connections that bind all generations.

The world may be spiraling out of control today. But, the prophecy provides the hope of a rising generation that will restore the balance between humans and the natural world, symbolizing a renewal of values and a return to ancestral wisdom.

The Create-Your-Own-Prophecy Exercise

Prophecies are meant to be predicted. It doesn't matter if it's a Native American shaman or a child doing the predicting. Shamans and prophets use their unique knowledge and powers to make a prophecy, but children can use their dreams and hopes to convert them into reality by prophesying them.

1. Take a pen and paper (or chalk and a blackboard if you have them) and write down how the world is right now. At the time of writing this, the coronavirus (COVID-19) has lessened a lot but still plagues many parts of the globe. There is a fierce war going on between Russia and Ukraine, and political and economic turmoil is experienced by almost every nation. Google every prominent problem that the world is facing right now.

2. Predict how the world should be instead of how it is. Should all the wars end? Should the coronavirus stop existing? Should there be harmony between all the nations in the world?

   Could humans learn to live with nature instead of destroying it? How about including technology in a harmonic community? Consider how the world needs to be instead of doing all the harmful things it is doing right now.

3. Discuss the prophecies with family and friends. What do they think about the predictions? Can they provide more effective means to realize a better future? They may have more innovative means of creating a fruitful prophecy.

4. Draw a simple picture of the resulting prophecy. Predicting harmony between the people and the environment could make a picture of a little girl hugging a formidable oak. A love for

animals can be emphasized by a boy playing with his pet dog. Educating technologically inclined people about nature and its importance can be depicted with an image of a child playing on a smartphone nestled under a tree.

The possibilities of creating a prophecy are endless, and its implications can make the world a better place for many generations.

Chapter 6: Celebrating Nature

The wind blew gently, like someone speaking softly in Muata's ear. It carried the earthy smell of ancient trees and dirt. Sunlight peeked through the leaves above, making flickering shapes dance on the ground like sunlight on water. The young boy wasn't just standing in the forest; he felt completely surrounded by it. It was like a world that was alive, full of secrets waiting to be discovered.

Muata wasn't just standing in any ordinary forest. For generations, their people had walked hand-in-hand with this ancient place. Here, whispers of the past lingered in the rustling leaves. Elders spoke of spirits who waltzed in crackling firelight, their wisdom carried on the wind. Powerful creatures, guardians of the mountains, were more than just bedtime stories – they were the very essence of this land. Respecting it wasn't a duty; it was a thrilling pact. Understanding its rhythms was an adventure on its own, waiting to be unraveled. Living in harmony with nature meant they weren't just focused on surviving; this was how they lived their lives. To the Native Americans, nature is like a living legend, waiting to be embraced by those brave enough to listen.

To the Native Americans, nature is like a living legend, waiting to be embraced by those brave enough to listen.

The morning sun had a mischievous glint in its eye as it peeked through the ancient trees. It stood high in the sky, painting patterns on Muata's worn leather satchel. Today wasn't just any day. Today, the forest hummed with a promise whispered in the wind. The boy was so excited, and anticipation bubbled in the boy's chest like a hidden spring!

In his hand, his trusty sketchbook felt less like paper and more like a portal, which was about to filled with the magic his Grandma would unleash through stories. They weren't just stories to be heard – they were an invitation, a chance to peek behind the veil of everyday life and see the extraordinary. Today, Muata would be listening to tales of the forest's power and the animals' wisdom; he'd become part of them; his heart was a blank page ready to be inscribed with the reverence his people held for this incredible world. With each skip along the familiar path, the forest floor crunched under his eager steps, and the very Earth seemed to beckon him deeper into the waiting wonder.

Finally, Grandma's cottage came into sight from the forest's emerald embrace. Smoke curled from its chimney, promising warmth and the comforting scent of woodsmoke and freshly baked bread. As Muata burst through the weathered wooden door, a wave of familiar warmth washed over him. The air hummed with the gentle hum of the old rocking chair by the fireplace, and the room was bathed in a golden glow emanating from the crackling fire.

There, nestled in her tiny cot by the hearth, sat Grandma. Her face, etched with the wisdom of years spent in communion with the land, cradled a warm smile as she saw him. Her eyes sparkled with the promise of an adventure waiting to unfold. Muata's heart thumped a happy rhythm. He scrambled across the worn wooden floor, his satchel clutched tightly in his hand and settled himself onto the small stool beside her cot. He was ready. The tales of some legends were waiting, and Grandma held the key.

Grandma's voice, raspy with age yet strangely captivating, filled the room, weaving a spell with each word. The older woman cleared her throat and started with a smile on her face.

The Raven and the Stolen Light – A Tlingit Legend

There was a raven called Kit-ka'ositiyi-qa-yit, which means "Son of Kit-ka'ositiyi-qa."
Copetersen www.copetersen.com, CC BY-SA 3.0 <https://creativecommons.org/licenses/by-sa/3.0>, via Wikimedia Commons:
https://commons.wikimedia.org/wiki/File:3782_Common_Raven_in_flight.jpg

"Sit still, little one," she began, her eyes twinkling like distant stars. "Let me tell you a tale of a time before time. In the beginning, there was a being called Raven. He was called Kit-ka'ositiyi-qa-yit, which means "Son of Kit-ka'ositiyi-qa." After several tries, he created the world, but it was a blanket of endless nights. Not a single star dared peek, and not a sliver of moon was anywhere to be seen. Darkness, thick as bear fur, clung to everything."

She paused, taking a sip from a steaming mug held in her hands. Muata leaned in, anticipation buzzing in his veins.

Her voice dropped to a whisper, sending shivers down Muata's spine. "There was a powerful guardian – a grumpy fellow. He was living in a large house far up the hill. He had a cold heart. The guardian kept the stars, moon, and even the sun locked away in a box, jealously keeping the light for himself." She shook her head.

"Our people were lost, groping and fumbling in the dark because of the guardian's greed. Raven, bless his clever soul, couldn't bear to see their plight. He was never one to shy away from a challenge, so it didn't take long for him to devise a cunning trick. So, he hatched a plan – a daring one that would forever change the face of the world."

"This grumpy guardian, he had a daughter. And what did Raven do? He shrunk himself down to be smaller than a teardrop. Mmhmmm. He turned himself into something as tiny as dirt and jumped into the woman's favorite glass cup. She drank of the cup and became pregnant." Grandma chuckled. Muata's eyes widened, picturing the trickster in his mind.

"When Raven grew into a babe, he found the shelf where the guardian kept his treasures. The baby, him being Raven in disguise, of course, cried for everything he could see. "Shiny!" he'd yell, pointing at the objects stacked high in the corner for three days. Each day, when the guardian couldn't take the wailing any longer, he brought down those boxes and gave them to the lad just to quiet the little Raven down one by one."

Raven let out the stars.

Grandma's eyes gleamed with amusement. "What do you think Raven did with the boxes, Muata? He first let out the stars and then the moon up the smoke hole. They both shot into the sky before anyone could blink. But, the Raven kept the last box with himself for a while after escaping."

"One day, he heard of a man who guarded a well with abundant water, so he decided to trick him as well. He turned himself into the man's brother-in-law and drank all the water until it was almost finished. He tried to escape when the man caught him but got stuck in the smoke hole. The man got angry, so he made a fire under the Raven while he hung in the smoke hole, unable to fly away. All that smoke from his fire turned Raven's feathers black as night."

"Raven finally escaped, spitting water here and there. That was how he created the great rivers of the world. He landed in a village, but the villagers tried to fight him for the last box that he had, so he opened the box, and the sun shot up into the sky. And, so our people were bathed in glorious light, a gift from the cleverest trickster the world had ever known."

She winked at Muata, a knowing glint in her eye. "So, you see, little one, even the smallest creature can hold the greatest courage. And sometimes, a little trickery can bring about the most beautiful light."

Glooscap and the Changing Seasons (A Mi'kmaq Tale)

The Mi'kmaq people believed that a mighty spirit named Glooscap roamed their land.

"Muata, scoot closer and let the firelight warm you up," his grandma said. "I have another tale for you." She adjusted herself in her chair.

"Long, long ago, in the land of the Mi'kmaq people, there, a mighty spirit named Glooscap roamed. He had great strength and wisdom. But, even Glooscap couldn't hold back the god of winter who sought to freeze the world." Muata's eyes widened. His grandma nodded, "Yes, indeed."

"One day, the crystal teeth of frost bit into the earth, turning colorful forests into brittle statues and rivers into ice. The Mi'kmaq people cried out. Glooscap's heart was heavy with the people's sorrow – he wouldn't give in. He kept fighting frost to frost with the god of winter until he could no longer do so."

"With a roar that shook the very mountains, he set off to find the god of summer – the spirit chased away by the god of winter's icy fist. His journey was long and harsh. But, Glooscap pushed on – his determination etching lines on his face, his eyes burning with the promise of spring."

"Finally, after a very long and difficult trip, Glooscap reached the god of summer's land. It was warm there, sunshine everywhere, unlike the freezing cold he'd just been in. He found Summer relaxing under beautiful flowers, wearing a crown made of sunlight." "When he spoke, Glooscap's voice was rough from the cold. He told the god of summer about the Mi'kmaq people and how the god of winter had made their land all icy. Glooscap's voice showed how much he cared about his people, and he really wanted things to be normal again with the four seasons."

"The god of summer saw how upset Glooscap was and felt bad for him. He stood up and smiled kindly. He was touched by Glooscap's bravery and humility. Then, he, the god of summer, waved his hand, and the cold winter chill disappeared. A soft wind blew across Mi'kma'ki, and the first spring flowers started to bloom, melting away the frost. The four seasons were back in order, just like before, all thanks to Glooscap's bravery."

These stories remind us that nature is so much more than just the ground we walk on.
Jessie Eastland, CC BY-SA 4.0 <https://creativecommons.org/licenses/by-sa/4.0>, via Wikimedia Commons: https://commons.wikimedia.org/wiki/File:Desert_Electric.jpg

These stories remind us that nature is so much more than just the ground we walk on. It's like one big, living storybook filled with lessons and adventures scattered across the pages within. The Raven's cleverness showed how we should be confident in ourselves. Even the smallest person can make a big impact. Glooscap's journey taught us the importance of balance and respect for the changing seasons. Like both of these legends, we can build a special connection with nature even by simply stepping outside and feeling the sunshine on our faces. Amazing things happen all around us every single day. So, next time you're feeling curious, step outside, explore, and celebrate the incredible world we share with all living things.

Activity

Nature Appreciation Journal

Are you ready to take your love for nature to the next level? Grab your hat and sunscreen - we're going outside to see the wonders of nature!

What Is a Nature Appreciation Journal?

It serves as a place to record all of your outside senses—hearing, seeing, smelling, and feeling.

Did you find a feathery surprise that a squirrel left behind? Did the wind whisper secrets through the leaves? Jot it all down!

1. **Step 1:** Find a notebook you like, colorful or plain, big or small. Something you can write and draw in.

2. **Step 2:** Grab your favorite pencils, markers, crayons, or paints. If you like drawing outside, bring a clipboard or something hard to write on.

3. **Step 3:** Lace up those hiking boots and head outside, whether in your backyard or a nearby park. Take a deep breath and soak in the sights, sounds, and smells of nature all around you.

4. **Step 4:** Take a closer look. Pay attention to everything around you. See the shapes of leaves, the colors of flowers, and how tree bark feels. Listen to birds chirping, leaves blowing, and maybe even a stream trickling. Feel the wind, smell the dirt after a rain, and listen to all the sounds around you.

5. **Step 5:** Use your paper and pencil. To let everyone around you know what you experienced, record in writing or drawing everything you saw, heard, smelled, tasted, and felt.

   Write about animals, plants, or places you saw. Draw pictures, write poems, stories, or how you felt about being outside. Set your imagination free.

6. **Step 6:** Observe the changes that happen over time. Return to the same spot outside and see how it changes with the seasons. Look for spring flowers, summer leaves, pretty fall colors, etc.

7. **Step 7:** As you spend time outdoors and fill your journal with your own unique observations and creations, take a moment to reflect on your experiences. How did it feel to connect with nature on a deeper level? What did you learn about yourself and the world around you?

8. **Step 8:** Your discoveries are not meant for your eyes alone. Once you've filled your nature appreciation journal with all your amazing observations and experiences, share your findings with the people around you. Sharing your journal is not only a way to connect with friends, family, or classmates, but it's also an opportunity to inspire each other to explore and appreciate the wonders of nature even more.

9. **Step 9:** Keep exploring, observing, and filling your nature appreciation journal with discoveries and insights. With each new adventure, you'll deepen your connection with nature and gain a

greater appreciation for its stories and lessons.

So, what are you waiting for? Grab your journal and head outside to embark on your next great adventure. Allow nature to teach you its ways, and the world will become your personal playground.

Chapter 7: Trickster Tales

Native American tales aren't all about magic, nature, and spiritual ancestors. They are a collection of fascinating trickster tales that have people laughing their heads off while learning a useful thing or two. They are stories of cunningness, wisdom, bravery, and stupidity, but they also give you unexpected morals you can live by. It's time to outsmart the smartest tricksters in Native American folklore and learn a few good things in the process.

The Coyote and the Rattlesnake

A lone coyote feeling refreshed after having a drink at the pool.
California Department of Fish and Wildlife from Sacramento, CA, USA, CC BY 2.0

A rattlesnake is considered to be the wisest of the wise.

As far as the eye can see, the landscape stretched out into an endless expanse of barrenness. The Earth was a tapestry of shifting sands, ranging in color from golden yellows to deep reds, moving up and down in graceful curves and dunes sculpted by the relentless winds.

The sky above was a brilliant blue, uninterrupted by clouds for days on end. The sun beat down relentlessly on the rolling sands and (surprisingly) the considerable patches of vegetation that had sustained wildlife in the arid region for generations. A sheet of water reflecting the blue sky glimmered blissfully in the distance, and just beyond that, a row of snow-capped peaks were faintly visible, lining the expanse.

Despite the beauty of the desert and the unexpected sources of food and water available, a lone coyote could be seen ambling up a large dune, feeling refreshed after having a drink at the pool. No other animals were visible for miles around, at least on the surface.

A multitude of lizards were nestled in their hidey holes beneath the sand, their worn-out scales craving for a bit of sun and water. Snakes slithered through the underbrush, their sinuous forms disappearing into the shadows. Birds of prey were seen as indiscernible dots on the horizon, never daring to circle near the coyote.

Who was this coyote that formidable creatures like lizards, snakes, and vultures preferred to hide from rather than come near him? He wasn't a fearsome beast but looked more like a frailer, smaller version of a wolf. He barely had any sharp teeth or claws. His fur was decaying, and his body had lost its original strength. He was getting old, after all.

However, the coyote's eyes sparkled with cunningness and malice. Indeed, it was his brain and wit that made him the most intimidating animal in the land. He was the sliest of the sly, outsmarting anyone and everyone who crossed his path and stealing their most prized possessions.

All living creatures in the beautiful desert had learned to avoid him like the plague, including humans, the apex predator, and the most intelligent of all animals.

"It seemed not all creatures had learned their lesson," the coyote thought, for when he reached the top of the dune, he could see something slither toward him over the sand below – someone whose head glittered in the afternoon sun. As it crawled nearer, he could see it was a snake holding a dazzling golden gem on its head.

"Ha, another snake!" thought the coyote. He seemed new in the desert. "Look at him flaunting his shiny gem. It's mesmerizing and beautiful. I want it. I'll have it. Let him come!"

However, the slithering creature, now climbing the dune on which the coyote stood, wasn't just any snake. He was a rattlesnake, considered to be the wisest of the wise, whom nobody had managed to outsmart so far. But he was also kind, compassionate, and quick to forgive.

The coyote didn't know all this, and when the rattlesnake arrived at the top, the sly old animal greeted him with a fake smile: "How are you, my dear friend? What is that thing on your head?"

"I'm good. Thank you for asking, friend," the rattlesnake replied. "I came all the way from those snow-covered mountains beyond the lake. Oh, and this is my precious gem – a symbol of knowledge and power."

"It's magnificent!" the coyote said with a hint of greed. Quickly realizing it, he tried to cover it up by saying, "Come now. You must be tired after the long journey. Unload your burden and take some rest in the shadow of this dune on the other side."

"Thank you, I will. I'll leave the gem buried just beneath the sand here so it doesn't attract greedy eyes. Will you stand guard over it, please?"

"I'll guard it with my life!" the coyote promised eagerly.

"Thank you! You're too kind," said the rattlesnake gratefully. Then, he dug up a small part of the sand, placed his gem in the hollow, and covered it up with the surrounding sand again. Crawling to the other side of the dune, he slept soundly in its shadow.

The coyote couldn't contain his excitement. "This was too easy," he thought. "I didn't even need to use my cunningness. Fool of a snake. I'll take really good care of his gem, back in my cave. But first, I need to make sure he is asleep."

He crept down to where the rattlesnake lay and closely monitored his breathing. After a couple of hours, his breathing stabilized as he began to snore. The coyote crept back up the slope and greedily started digging the sand in the exact spot where the gem lay buried.

Several minutes passed, but he couldn't see the sparkling gem. "This is strange," he thought. "The foolish snake hadn't buried it too deep." To the west, the sun was about to set, but he kept digging, getting more and more impatient. Minutes turned to hours, and the small hollow became a large hole on top of the dune, but he still hadn't found the precious gem.

It was dark outside, and the hole was getting deeper, but the coyote had eyes only for the gem, so he continued to dig. Finally, he reached hard ground beneath the sand, and he could dig no further. That was when he decided to give up, thinking the gem was lost.

For the first time since he had begun digging, he looked up. Night had turned to day, but he could only see a tiny dot of the morning sky above; that was how deep he had dug himself. He tried to climb up, but he couldn't get a grip on the towering wall of sand. It kept slipping from his paws.

Just as he was about to give up and resign himself to his fate, he noticed a dark spot in the opening above. It was the head of the snake he had tried to dupe. He shouted up to him, "Help!"

"Why did you dig a hole so deep? Were you trying to find my gem?" The rattlesnake asked.

The coyote sheepishly replied, "Yes."

"Did you find it?"

"No."

The snake chuckled, and his head vanished from the opening. The coyote was afraid. Was the snake so angry with him that he had left him to rot in the hole? As dark thoughts consumed him, the snake's head popped in the opening again. This time, there wasn't just one but a dozen heads looking down at the coyote.

They were all the snakes he had outsmarted and stolen from in the desert. They were coiling their heads and tails around each other, and within moments, they had formed a long rope of snakes. The coyote gave a sigh of relief when the foremost snake who jumped in the hole (dragging the others down) was able to reach the bottom.

The rattlesnake was the last one holding the rest from above, and when the coyote held tight to the bottommost snake, he pulled the makeshift rope and dragged everyone up to the surface. When the coyote was out of the hole, he stammered his thanks to everyone and said to the rattlesnake, "I'm sorry I tried to take your gem and for losing it, too."

The rattlesnake tricked the coyote with a piece of ice crystal that he carved from a cave.
Danielarapava, CC BY-SA 4.0 <https://creativecommons.org/licenses/by-sa/4.0>, via Wikimedia Commons: https://commons.wikimedia.org/wiki/File:Frostedbubble2.jpg

The rattlesnake laughed and said, "Oh, but it was never a gem to begin with. It was just a piece of ice crystal I had carved from a cave in those snow-capped mountains. If you weren't so consumed by greed when you first saw it and took me for a fool, you might have noticed the water trailing off its sides as it slowly melted from the heat.

"Your sinister reputation had reached us animals up there. I knew you would try to take the gem at the first opportunity. By the time you started digging for it, it had completely melted into water, so you found nothing there. Any normal animal would have left it at that, but your greed prompted you to dig yourself deeper into the hole."

Indeed, the outsmarter was outsmarted. At the same time, the coyote was humbled. He realized that true wisdom lies in knowing that others are equally wise. Despite their grievances, the other snakes came to help him, which made him respect every living creature. The experience transformed the cunning trickster into a wise animal.

The Raven's Moonlit Dance

Many of the Native American tribes believe the coyote to be the trickster, but the majority of them hail the raven as the god of tricks.

The majority of the Native American tribes hail the raven as the god of tricks.
Keppler, Udo J., 1872-1956, artist; Poe, Edgar Allan, 1809-1849. Raven., Public domain, via Wikimedia Commons:
https://commons.wikimedia.org/wiki/File:%22FREE_SILVER%22_raven_art_in_1900_detail,_fr om-_Nevermore_-_Keppler._LCCN2010651343_(cropped).tif

A mischievous raven lived in the heart of the dense forest, where the moon's silver light dances through the leaves. He was known far and wide for his cunning ways and his insatiable desire for beauty. He often dreamed of attending the grand forest gathering, where creatures from all corners of the woods would gather to celebrate the full moon.

On a full moon night, as he perched atop a mighty oak, he gazed at his plain black feathers and longed for the colorful hues of the other birds. Determined to stand out at the gathering, he devised a cunning plan. He would adorn himself with the most exquisite feathers stolen from his fellow birds.

He flew from tree to tree, charming his way into the birds' trust with sweet words and promises of friendship. And, one by one, he plucked feathers from their plumage, leaving behind a trail of betrayal and sorrow.

Adorned with feathers of every color imaginable, the raven made his way to the grand gathering, his heart swelling with pride at the sight of his magnificent disguise. But, as he entered the clearing, he was met with whispers and stares of disapproval from the other creatures.

Undeterred, he strutted into the gathering, eager to bask in the admiration of his peers. But, as the night unfolded, he began to feel a sense of unease creeping into his heart. Despite his elaborate disguise, he couldn't shake the feeling of emptiness that gnawed at his soul.

As the hours passed and the moon reached its zenith, he found himself drawn to a quiet corner of the clearing where a wise old owl sat in silent contemplation. Intrigued, the raven approached the creature.

"What ails you, raven?" the owl asked, fixing him with a knowing gaze.

"I sought to be admired and celebrated, but instead, I feel only shame and regret," the raven confessed sadly.

The wise owl revealed that true beauty lies in the authenticity of our hearts.
https://pixabay.com/illustrations/owl-branch-perch-wise-wisdom-bird-6164884/

The owl nodded and spread his wings to reveal his glory. "True beauty lies not in the adornments we wear but in the authenticity of our hearts," he said softly. "You are a creature of the night, raven, and your true beauty shines brightest when you embrace your own nature."

With a heavy heart, the raven realized the folly of his vanity. He returned to his nest in the cliffs and shed his stolen feathers. That moonlit night, he had found a new sense of freedom in his authenticity as he began to accept himself the way he was. He soared across the heavens, spreading his black wings, knowing that true beauty could only be found in the depths of one's own heart.

Two Truths and a Lie

Each question below is based on the two stories above. Each question has three options — two are true, and one is a lie. Choose the lie to score points!

1. **Which animals were in the desert?**

   - Lizards
   - Foxes
   - Snakes

2. **Who hid from the coyote?**

   - Lizards
   - Vultures
   - Snakes

Hint: They didn't come near the coyote, but they weren't exactly hiding from him.

3. **What did the coyote want from the rattlesnake?**

   - He wanted the rattlesnake's head.
   - He wanted to outsmart the rattlesnake.
   - He wanted the rattlesnake's gem.

4. **What was the moral of the coyote's story?**

   - To respect every living creature
   - The wise were those who considered everyone wise
   - To know that vanity is a folly

5. **What was the raven known for?**

   - His insatiable desire for beauty
   - His wisdom
   - His cunningness

6. **What did the owl say to the raven?**

   - True beauty lies in the adornments we wear.
   - True beauty shines brightest upon embracing one's nature.
   - True beauty is in the authenticity of our hearts.

7. **What did the raven do after going back to his nest?**

   - Shed his stolen feathers
   - Spread his black wings
   - Failed to realize his folly

Chapter 8: The Whispering Winds: Stories of Adventure

The Native Americans have been adoring, worshiping, and living in nature for eons, and with nature comes adventure. Their tales are far different, more thrilling, unimaginably magical, and even more adventurous than the regular adventure stories of other civilizations. Their folklore unravels many mysteries of nature and embodies the spirit of exploration and bravery in the unlikeliest of places.

The Native Americans have been adoring, worshiping, and living in nature for eons.
https://www.pexels.com/photo/photo-of-stream-during-daytime-3225517/

The Journey of Falling Star

In some Native American tales, Falling Star refers to a legendary figure who fell from the heavens to save the world from falling into chaos. In others, he is a young warrior blessed with the spirit of the wild and the wisdom of his ancestors. In every story, however, he is a curious hero with a thirst for adventure.

One of the tales portrayed a unique natural world where forests were as old as the Earth and mountains touched the sky. The ever-flowing waters of the rivers showed the dazzling beauty of their depths, and all animals, birds, and insects existed in perfect harmony with each other.

In such a wonderful world, there lived a young warrior named Falling Star. He was renowned not only for his skill in battle but also for his deep love for nature and his unquenchable thirst for knowledge. However, he didn't venture far from the confines of the forest where he lived, not for lack of curiosity, but because he loved his family even more.

One evening, as he sat beneath a large oak with his eyes closed, listening to the gentle rustle of leaves and the distant calls of night owls, an elder interrupted his reverie to share a tale of a legendary flower.

"There is a flower of wisdom that is said to bloom only once every hundred years. Tomorrow marks its day of blooming."

The flower of wisdom is said to bloom only once every hundred years.
Devaprasanna Ghatak, CC BY 4.0 <https://creativecommons.org/licenses/by/4.0>, via Wikimedia Commons:
https://commons.wikimedia.org/wiki/File:Spectacularly_colourful_canna_flower_rising_into_a_cloudy_sky.jpg

"What is so special about this flower apart from the hundred-year blooming period?" asked Falling Star. "Is it beautiful to behold? Does it have a captivating smell?"

"It is all that and more," replied the elder. "Rumors abound that whoever possesses its petals will be granted unparalleled wisdom and a singular insight into how the world works."

Falling Star was fascinated by the prospect of such vast knowledge, and his family encouraged him to seek the flower. He had finally found his calling, and amid many tearful goodbyes and promises to return with the flower, he embarked on a quest to find it. With his trusty blade at his side and a determined heart, he ventured into the unknown.

His journey led him through dense forests where the trees were as old as time itself, and the trickling streams held water so pure that their flow created a sweet melody. Each step brought new challenges, from treacherous ravines to slippery cliffs. Yet, he also encountered friendly faces, as a great white stag helped him back on the right path when he took a wrong turn, and an enigmatic owl accompanied him in the dead of night.

As he ascended the rugged slopes of towering mountains, battling fierce winds and biting cold, Falling Star marveled at the majesty of the world around him. At first, he was daunted by the tall peaks shrouded in clouds and the sheer extremity of the elements (heavy rains that felt like hailstorms and fierce winds that almost swept him over the edge of cliffs). Eventually, he learned to respect the raw power of nature, finding beauty in its harshest landscapes and wisdom in its untamed wilderness.

Through perseverance and determination, he finally reached the summit of the tallest peak, where legend spoke of the magical flower's hidden sanctuary. There, amid a carpet of colorful blooms and crystalline waters, he beheld the fabled flower, its petals glowing with an ethereal light.

With trembling hands, Falling Star plucked a single petal, feeling a surge of ancient wisdom course through his veins. It was like he was holding the weight of the entire world in his hands, yet it felt as light as a feather. At that moment, he understood the true meaning of knowledge – not as a prize to be won but a journey to be embraced. It was an unquenchable thirst that needed to be filled from time to time, just like a water bottle.

Falling Star's journey taught him the value of perseverance and respect for nature.

As he descended from the mountain, cradling the precious petal close to his heart, Falling Star quietly reflected on his journey. His quest had granted him a deeper insight into the natural world. It had taught him the value of perseverance, respect for nature, and the boundless power of the human spirit to seek knowledge in the face of unprecedented dangers. And, though his journey had ended, and he was about to return home, his quest for knowledge would continue.

Echoes of the Canyon

It is said that the whispers of the wind carry echoes of the past, voices of Native American ancestors that reverberate across massive mountain ranges and deep canyons. One such tale narrates the adventure of a young girl named Whispering Wind.

In the quiet expanse of a forgotten forest, where sunlight streamed and twinkled through the trees and the wind whistled over the grass, there lived a young girl named Whispering Wind. She was unlike the other children of her village – her eyes always alight with curiosity and her spirit as wild as the wind itself.

Every evening, her grandmother told her tales of history and adventure, of her ancestors and the natural world at the beginning of time. Unfortunately, there came a time when she had exhausted all her stories and didn't have any new ones to tell. Seeing the dejected look on Whispering Wind's face, she said, "Legend says there is a hidden canyon south of here that echoes with voices of the past. It never runs out of fantastical tales which also happen to be true."

Legend says there is a hidden canyon south of here that echoes with voices of the past.

"Won't it be dangerous? They sound like ghosts," said Whispering Wind apprehensively.

"The unknown speaks of dangers untold. Can your curiosity overcome your fear?"

"I don't know."

"Then, go find out."

And so, Whispering Wind ventured southward, deeper into the forest than she had ever gone before. The trees were so thick that barely any sunlight trickled through. It was always dark as the night, but still, she plodded on. The path, which she could hardly see, was winding and treacherous. She stumbled and fell several times, but she got back up each time and continued her journey.

After several days that seemed like years, she arrived at the edge of a wide canyon. It stretched before her like a yawning chasm, its depths shrouded in a thick fog and an even thicker mystery. Despite its daunting presence, she felt an irresistible pull drawing her closer, beckoning her to explore its secrets.

With each step she took, the air seemed to hum with the echoes of a thousand voices . . . faint whispers carried on the breeze. Whispering Wind may have braved the dangerous path that led her there, but she was too afraid to carry on any further. Nevertheless, her curiosity took the better of her, and she longed to know what the voices were saying. The echoes felt like an enchanting melody of knowledge and history that soothed all her fears and gave her courage. Eventually, she descended into the depths of the canyon, her heart pounding with excitement.

As she ventured deeper, the whispers grew louder and clearer, swirling around her like a whirlwind of memories. With each passing moment, she felt herself being transported back in time to a world where her ancestors roamed the land and their stories echoed through the ages.

"He was a gifted horse trainer who tamed the wildest beasts..."

"She was a fierce warrior against whom the strongest men felt weak..."

Whispering Wind listened with rapt attention as the voices of the past filled the canyon, narrating a tapestry of tales that spanned generations. There was a group of brave warriors who fought valiantly to protect their people, wise elders who passed down ancient wisdom, and bold adventurers who explored uncharted territories in search of new land.

But, amid the tales of heroism and triumph, she also heard whispers of sorrow and loss – of battles fought and lives sacrificed in the name of freedom and justice. And, with each story she heard, she gained a deeper understanding of the struggles and hardships that had shaped her heritage.

Despite the dark nature of some of the tales, Whispering Wind felt a sense of pride and honor for the legacy that had been passed down to her. She experienced her ancestors' courage and resilience course through her veins, guiding her forward as she walked the path they had paved before her.

As the sun was about to set, casting a dull glow across the canyon walls, Whispering Wind climbed back up from the depths with a newfound sense of purpose. She knew that she carried with her the stories of her ancestors, their wisdom, courage, losses, and triumphs – her history, in short.

Her journey back home was spent in profound reflection. She realized that the echoes of the hidden canyon may have been ghosts, but she was no longer afraid of them. If anything, she felt closer to her family's heritage and traditions. She knew she was no longer just a girl wandering through the forest – she had become a guardian of that heritage, a keeper of the stories that had shaped her identity.

Armed with the power of history, she was ready to face whatever challenges lay ahead.
https://pixabay.com/illustrations/native-american-native-american-women-8076731/

As she looked out at the world stretching before her, she knew that she was ready to face whatever challenges lay ahead, armed with the power of history, the curiosity that had led her to the mystical place, and the unwavering belief in the value of self-discovery. In the echoes of the past, Whispering Wind had found her roots and the strength to do good things and accomplish great wonders in the future. For one, she would be telling stories to her grandmother, not the other way around.

Create Your Own Adventure Story

Adventure stories are highly inspirational. They motivate people not just to go for an adventure of their own but also to create their own adventure story. This simple activity only requires a notebook, a pen, imagination, and a thirst for adventure. Here's an example to start with:

Once upon a time, in the heart of a forest, there lived a young boy. His village was in the middle of a vast clearing, surrounded by all kinds of trees and wildlife.

One day, his grandfather called him to his hut and told him of a sacred totem hidden deep within the forest. He said that it was the key to unlocking the wisdom of their ancestors.

Prompt 1: The Journey Begins

Accompanied by his loyal wolf companion, the young boy set out on his quest to find the sacred totem. Along the way, he encountered a gushing river blocking his path. How does he overcome this obstacle?

Prompt 2: Trial of the Forest Spirits

As he went deeper into the forest, he stumbled upon mysterious spirits dancing in the moonlight. To proceed, he must prove his worthiness by completing a task. What challenges do they present to him?

Prompt 3: Encounter with the Wise Owl

Guided by the whispers of the wind, the young boy came upon a wise old owl perched high in the branches of an ancient oak tree. The owl offered him cryptic advice that would aid him on his journey. What is that advice?

Prompt 4: The Guardians of the Sacred Totem

At long last, he reached the heart of the forest where the sacred totem lay. But, before he could claim it, he must face the guardians – spirits of the ancestors tasked with protecting their legacy. How does he prove himself worthy of their trust?

Prompt 5: The Return Home

With the sacred totem in hand, the young boy embarked on the journey back to his village, where his grandfather awaited his return. Along the way, he reflected on the lessons he learned and the challenges he overcame. How has his journey changed him, and what wisdom will he share with his people?

As he reached his village with the sacred totem held high, he was ready to embrace his role as a guardian of his tribe's heritage and a keeper of the spirit of the sacred totem.

In essence, the main character should first be described.

1. Where do they live? What is their personality like?

2. The secondary characters should be shown. How do all these characters interact with each other?

3. The adventure should be introduced in their dialogue. What kind of magic does the quest contain?

4. As the journey begins, the challenges need to be stated, followed by how the main character overcomes them.

5. The story should conclude with a reflection on the main character. What did they learn from the adventure?

Chapter 9: Fireside Fables: Tales of Belonging

In the olden days, during seasons with long nights, under flickering lights or dancing flames, the natives would gather and share stories. But these weren't ordinary stories; they were fables and tales that have been passed down from generation to generation. These tales are usually full of adventures, wisdom, and a powerful feeling of belonging.

Fables shed light on matters that are close to the heart – things like the search for a place to fit in and the courage it takes to be one's self.

Fables aren't just for entertainment. They speak of things that concern us as humans and our surroundings. They shed light on matters close to the heart – things like the search for a place to fit in, the courage it takes to be one's self, and the importance of family and friends. These stories reveal how we are all connected to something bigger than ourselves. They teach us to appreciate Mother Earth even further.

Through these tales, the profound connection Native American cultures hold with their communities is uncovered, as well as the intricate dance of forging identity and the enduring spirit that seeks to find its rightful place within the grand threads of existence. The unwavering strength of legendary heroes and the whispers of ancestral spirits who guide us all on this timeless quest are highly spoken of. As we immerse ourselves in these stories, we are bound to get a deeper understanding of ourselves and the inherent human need for connection, and when the final word is spoken, it never fails to leave a lasting resonance within us long after the story is told.

This last chapter includes more fables and tales that reflect the search for identity, belonging, and community. Are you up for a few more stories? Well, you won't be disappointed. The tales of Awena, The Healer, and the Legend of Chief Seattle are laid out here for you.

You're on the last lap – keep reading, champ!

Awena the Healer

Once upon a time, in the Navajo land, there lived a curious girl named Awena. After the death of her mother, Awena struggled to find her place in her tribe. She knew she had the potential to do great things, but discovering what they were was difficult. Finally, she decided to go in search of the legendary Spider Woman. She had been told of the legend as a child and believed the being could help her.

Awena climbed a sacred mountain to find her purpose, her heart pounding with anticipation.

One night, under the desert stars, Awena climbed a sacred mountain to find her purpose, her heart pounding with anticipation. At the top, she met an old woman, her skin etched with time and her eyes full of wisdom. It was the Spider Woman. She looked at the young girl and could sense why she came. "Child," Spider Woman said, her voice as gentle as a breeze. "You seek your purpose, but it lies within." Awena's heart hammered in her chest. "Your purpose lies not in what you chase, but in the gifts you already hold," the old woman continued, "you have a keen eye for herbs, a gentle touch with the sick, and a spirit that resonates with the Earth. Your purpose, child, is to be a healer, a bridge between your tribe and the land."

A wave of clarity washed over Awena. The visions and encounters that had been plaguing her – they weren't random. They were a reflection of her true self, leading her toward her destiny.

The legend took the girl in and began to groom her. She told Awena that everyone and everything is like a thread in a giant web. Awena listened, her heart swelling. She learned that every choice and every action rippled through the web. Kindness mended frayed strands while greed unraveled them. The land, the animals, the people - they were kin, bound by invisible threads.

Awena learned that patience was an important virtue to possess. Spider Woman showed her how to mend broken threads and how to honor the delicate balance. As days turned into weeks, Spider-Woman taught Awena the ways of a healer. She taught the young woman to be courageous, compassionate, and resilient. And so, Awena discovered her purpose: to be a healer.

She returned to the tribe, no longer a lost girl but a woman with a purpose. Her touch soothed wounds, and her knowledge of herbs brought comfort. She was told of a man sick to death, and she decided to pay him a visit.

Awena healing old man Herrick.

Old man Herrick, a respected elder, lay shivering with a fever, his coughs echoing through the longhouse. Awena clutched her pouch of herbs, each one gathered under the watchful eye of Spider Woman. She placed a cool hand on his forehead. Closing her eyes, Awena whispered a prayer to Spider Woman, the creator. Memories of her lessons flooded back – the soothing touch of yucca root and the calming scent of lavender, and she got to work.

By morning, the fever had broken. A weak smile graced Herrick's lips as he looked at Awena: "You are a weaver, too, child," he rasped, "weaving health back into tired bodies." Awena's heart swelled. She wasn't just a healer – just like Spider-Woman, she was mending the tears in the web of life one person at a time.

The Legend of Chief Seattle

In the land of Native American tribes, Suquamish and Duwamish, a great leader was born. His name was Chief Seattle. Chief Seattle, or as he was sometimes called, Sealth, was a well-known and respected leader.

Chief Seattle, or as he was sometimes called, Sealth.
https://en.wikipedia.org/wiki/File:Chief_seattle.jpg

From his youth, whispers of the spirit world snaked through the rustling leaves and gurgling streams, forming a deep connection within him – to the land and his people. He listened to all the tales told by his elders, sagas of warriors and of spirits dwelling in every mountain peak and rushing waterway.

As years passed by for the legend, Chief Seattle walked the ancestral paths, absorbing the sacred rituals and traditions that were the lifeblood of his tribe. He honored the spirits that laid beneath the Earth, leaving offerings of fragrant tobacco and sweetgrass as a humble thank you for the bounty that sustained them.

But, Chief Seattle's vision stretched beyond the borders of his own tribe. He understood the unifying melody that bound all Native American hearts. He tirelessly stitched alliances and treaties, a bulwark against the people who sought to sever their connection to their ancestral lands.

One day, he gathered his people beneath a colossal cedar; its ancient boughs a protective canopy. As sunlight filtered through, dappling the faces of his tribe, Chief Seattle spoke. His voice was a deep rumble. He spoke of how all living things were connected and of the Earth as a sacred gift entrusted to them by the Great Spirit.

"Our ancestors walk beside us," he declared, his gaze sweeping across the rapt faces. "Their spirits are in the wind, guiding our every step. We honor them by treading lightly upon Mother Nature, making sure the delicate balance remains unbroken."

His words struck a chord within them, igniting a fierce sense of belonging and purpose. They understood – their identity was as inseparable from the land as the bark from the towering trees, and their traditions were woven into the very fabric of the natural world.

Under Chief Seattle's unwavering leadership, the tribe embraced their sacred duty as guardians of the Earth. With unwavering resolve, they protected the verdant forests and life-giving rivers that cradled their existence. They found strength in their shared heritage, drawing upon the wisdom of their ancestors to navigate the treacherous currents of a changing world.

Governor of Washington, Isaac Stevens, negotiated with Chief Seattle to sell the land, which is now the city of Seattle.

Sometime in 1854, when the territorial Governor of Washington, Isaac Stevens, visited their land, he negotiated with Chief Seattle for the sale of the land, which is now the city of Seattle. It was named in honor of the Chief. In response to the Governor, Chief Seattle gave his famous speech:

> *"How can you buy or sell the sky? The land? The idea is strange to us. If we do not own the freshness of the air and the sparkle of the water, how can you buy them? Every part of this earth is sacred to my people. Every shining pine needle, every sandy shore, every mist in the dark woods, every meadow, every humming insect. All are holy in the memory and experience of my people...*
>
> *If we sell you our land, remember that the air is precious to us, that the air shares its spirit with all the life it supports. The wind that gave our grandfather his first breath also received his last sigh. The wind also gives our children the spirit of life. So, if we sell you our land, you must keep it apart and sacred, a place where man can go to taste the wind that is sweetened by the meadow flowers. Will you teach your children what we have taught our children? That the earth is our mother? What befalls the earth befalls all the sons of the earth.*
>
> *This we know: the earth does not belong to man; man belongs to the earth. All things are connected like the blood that unites us*

all. Man did not weave the web of life; he is merely a strand in it. Whatever he does to the web, he does to himself. One thing we know: Our God is also your God. The earth is precious to Him and to harm the earth is to heap contempt on its Creator."

(Earth in Balance: Ecology and the Human Spirit, Gore 1992, 159)

A hush fell over the gathering as Chief Seattle's words hung heavy in the air. Some faces creased further in solemn reflection. The weight of his message settled deep within them – a truth resonating with the very core of their being. After all, their people had always lived in harmony with the land.

Chief Seattle's voice was a powerful echo of their own connection to the Earth. His words, carried on the wind, ignited a fire in the hearts of his people. This wasn't just a speech; it was a passionate plea to honor the land that sustained them.

The impact of his words reverberated far beyond that day. They became a timeless message – a beacon for generations to come. Chief Seattle's voice became a rallying cry for those who championed the environment – a powerful reminder of our responsibility to protect the Earth. His legacy continues to inspire countless individuals and movements – their voices rising in unison for the land and the rights of those who have always called it home.

Activity: End-of-Book Quiz

Instructions:

Choose the correct answer for each question. Feel free to refer back to the book for help. Once you've answered all the questions, check your answers to see how well you remember the inspiring stories of Native American culture and folklore.

Chapter 1

Who were the two powerful beings that were referred to as the cosmic mother and father?

    a. Sun and Moon

    b. Spider Woman and Tawa, the sun god

    c. Eagle and Bear

    d. Buffalo and Deer

Why did the Wampanoag people respect nature so much?

_____

_____

_____

_____

_____

Chapter 2

Who was a famous Native American leader known for his role in the Battle of Little Bighorn?

    a. Chief Sitting Bull

    b. Chief Seattle

    c. Sacagawea

    d. Geronimo

Chapter 3

What lessons did you learn from the tales about the stars?

_____

_____

_____

_____

_____

Chapter 4

Why was the buffalo important to many Native American tribes?

    a. It provided food, clothing, and shelter.

    b. It was a symbol of fear and danger.

    c. It was believed to possess magical powers.

    d. It was considered sacred and worshiped.

What is the symbolism of the buffalo's life cycle to the people of the Plains tribes?

    a. Laughter and child-bearing.

    b. Unity and abundance.

    c. Sacrifice and wisdom.

    d. Flowing rivers and green gardens.

Chapter 5

What is a prophecy?

a. A historical event.

b. A prediction of the future.

c. A religious ceremony.

d. A moral lesson.

Which Native American tribe is particularly associated with the prophecy of the Seventh Generation?

a. Cherokee

b. Iroquois

c. Navajo

d. Apache

Chapter 6

Why did the god of summer decide to help Glooscap and the Mi'kmaq people?

a. Glooscap was strong and mighty.

b. Glooscap sang him songs of praise.

c. Glooscap offered prayers and sacrifices.

d. Glooscap came to him in humility.

Chapter 7

Which two of these are famous trickster figures in Native American mythology known for their mischievous antics?

a. Raven

b. Coyote

c. Bear

d. Fox

What lesson do trickster tales often teach us?

a. The importance of honesty and integrity.

b. The consequences of greed and selfishness.

c. The value of hard work and perseverance.

d. The dangers of trusting strangers.

Chapter 8

What role do the winds play in many Native American stories?

a. They carry messages from the spirits.

b. They bring storms and disasters.

c. They guide travelers on their journeys.

d. They whisper secrets to those who listen.

What is a vision quest?

a. A journey to find lost treasure.

b. A quest for knowledge and understanding.

c. A search for a missing person.

d. A battle against supernatural forces.

Chapter 9

What lesson does the story of Chief Seattle teach us about belonging?

a. The importance of preserving cultural heritage.

b. The value of environmental stewardship.

c. The need for unity and cooperation.

d. All of the above.

Answer Key

Chapter 2

Test of Knowledge Answers:

1. Sitting Bull was named Jumping Badger after his birth. He earned the name Sitting Bull after striking one of the enemy warriors with a coup stick at 14.

2. General George Custer.

3. General Alfred Sully.

4. Tahlequah, Oklahoma.

5. Due to new laws that allowed the relocation of aboriginal tribes, promising them better opportunities in big cities.

6. Mankiller returned to her Cherokee home in Oklahoma by 1977.

Chapter 3

Shooting for the Stars Quiz Answers:

1. A
2. D
3. B
4. A
5. C
6. B

7. D
8. A
9. B
10. A

Chapter 4

True or False Answers:
1. False
2. True
3. True
4. False
5. False
6. True
7. False
8. True

Chapter 7

Two truths and a Lie Answers:
1. Foxes
2. Vultures
3. He wanted the rattlesnake's head
4. To know that vanity is a folly
5. His wisdom
6. True beauty lies in the adornments we wear
7. Failed to realize his folly

Chapter 9

End of Book Quiz Answers:
Questions from Chapter 1:
1. B.
2. They understood that nature is part of the Circle of Life.
Questions from Chapter 2:
1. A.

Questions from Chapter 3:

1. A.

Questions from Chapter 4:

1. C.
2. A.

Questions from Chapter 5:

1. B.
2. D.

Questions from Chapter 6:

1. D.

Questions from Chapter 7:

1. A and B.

Questions from Chapter 8:

1. A.
2. B

Conclusion

You've now reached the end of this exciting journey through Native American tales. Some of the stories you read spoke about people who lived long ago, settling down and growing crops or wandering around hunting and foraging for food and other necessities. They spoke different languages, had a colorful culture, and passed down many legends. From their tales, you learned how the Native Americans explained how the world came to be and which heroes they believed played a part in their early history.

You also read about some of the bravest acts of Native American heroes throughout history and where they found the courage to triumph when everything seemed lost. As you've learned, having a leader was just as important to Native tribes as it is and has been in every other world culture.

Besides its role in creation, the natural world (especially the sky and the earth) was also considered a powerful source of blessings. Native Americans have many tales about the stars, retelling how these shiny objects guided them through adventures.

Hunters, warriors, and farmers alike lived in close communities, and to form these communities, they took inspiration from nature. One of the main characters in forming their peaceful communities was the buffalo. This powerful animal was both a gift and a source of many lessons that were passed down through generations.

Native Americans always had unique ways of celebrating nature. They believed that, like the buffalo, many other creatures brought people gifts, blessings, and lessons. They taught people how to live together with nature and all the natural beings around them because they could all help each other out.

However, as you've learned, the Native tribes also knew how tricky some creatures could be. While the stories about cunning tricksters can also teach one to respect nature, they also show that sometimes you must be very careful about how you approach people.

Nature holds many mysteries, too, according to Native American tales. Some of these mysteries invite people to unforgettable adventures, while others can show a person how brave they can be when encountering an unexpected challenge.

Like everyone else in this world, the ancient tribes knew how important it was for a person to find a place where they could be happy. Their fables speak about young people embarking on the journey of learning to be the best versions of themselves while respecting their link to nature and other people.

Many of the lessons from these Native American tales can be applied today. People today can build relationships with nature and each other just as closely as their Native ancestors were taught to do. Whether it's your neighbors, friends, classmates, family members, teachers, pets, or your favorite place outdoors, there is always a way to form a connection with your surroundings. You just have to find the inspiration to reach out, and this book has given you a treasure trove of information on how to do that.

References

Aktá Lakota Museum & Cultural Center. (n.d.). The Legend of the White Buffalo Woman. Aktá Lakota Museum & Cultural Center. https://aktalakota.stjo.org/lakota-legends/white-buffalo-woman/

Americans, N. (n.d.). Biography: Sitting Bull | American Experience | PBS. Www.pbs.org. https://www.pbs.org/wgbh/americanexperience/features/oakley-sitting-bull/

Araminta, M. (2023, May 23). The Geography of Mi'kmaq Folklore. ArcGIS StoryMaps. https://storymaps.arcgis.com/stories/b0fca956f299408ba4b8c2e3d4a47995

Azure, L. B. (2016, February 22). Actualizing the Seventh Generation Prophecy: A Case Study in Teacher Education at a Tribal College. Tribal College Journal of American Indian Higher Education. https://tribalcollegejournal.org/actualizing-the-seventh-generation-prophecy-a-case-study-in-teacher-education-at-a-tribal-college

Bob, B. (2021). CHIEF SEATTLE'S LETTER. Csun.edu. https://www.csun.edu/~vcpsy00h/seattle.htm

Brando, E. (2010). Wilma Mankiller. National Women's History Museum. https://www.womenshistory.org/education-resources/biographies/wilma-mankiller

Brown, J. (2020, October 23). What Is the Story of Glooscap? – KnowledgeBurrow.com. Knowledgeburrow.com. https://knowledgeburrow.com/what-is-the-story-of-glooscap/

Caduto, M. J., & Bruchac, J. (1998). Keepers of Life: Discovering Plants through Native American Stories and Earth Activities for Children. Fulcrum Pub.

CBC. (2020, March 4). Who is Glooscap? He's kind, respectful, and big, says Mi'kmaw educator. CBC. https://www.cbc.ca/news/canada/nova-scotia/legend-of-glooscap-mi-kmaw-culture-columnist-trevor-sanipass-1.5484002

Christo, C. (2021, August 4). The Hopi Prophecies Are Coming True — Here's Why We Should Pay Attention. The Hill; The Hill. https://thehill.com/changing-america/opinion/566362-the-hopi-prophecies-are-coming-true-heres-why-we-should-pay

DeGuzman, K. (2020, September 12). What is a Fable — Definition, Examples & Characteristics. StudioBinder. https://www.studiobinder.com/blog/what-is-a-fable-definition/

Goble, P. (1998). The Lost Children: The Boys Who Were Neglected. Simon & Schuster Children's Publishing Division.

History.com Editors. (2009, November 16). Chief Seattle Dies Near the City Named for Him. HISTORY. https://www.history.com/this-day-in-history/chief-seattle-dies-near-the-city-named-for-him

History.com Editors. (2009, November 9). Sitting Bull. HISTORY; A&E Television Networks. https://www.history.com/topics/native-american-history/sitting-bull

Institute for Public Relations. (2021, October 22). Native American Pioneer Chief Seattle (c. 1786 – 1866) | Institute for Public Relations. Instituteforpr.org. https://instituteforpr.org/native-american-pioneer-chief-seattle/

Jo, M. (2020, August 12). Learn More about the Legend of Chief Seattle - Discovering Washington State. Discovering Washington State. https://www.discoveringwashingtonstate.com/learn-more-about-the-legend-of-chief-seattle/

Judson L., M. (2004, April 28). The Raven in Native American Mythology. Judson L Moore. https://www.judsonlmoore.com/the-raven-in-native-american-mythology

Judson, K. (2004, October 9). Native American Stories (Myth-Folklore Online). Mythfolklore.net. https://www.mythfolklore.net/3043mythfolklore/reading/california/pages/06.htm

Keim, F. (n.d.). Marshall Cultural Atlas. Www.ankn.uaf.edu. http://www.ankn.uaf.edu/NPE/CulturalAtlases/Yupiaq/Marshall/raven/RavenStealsTheLight.html

Mall, L. (2018, February 12). Greatest Lakota Leaders Who Ever Lived – Lakota Mall. Lakota Mall. https://www.lakotamall.com/greatest-lakota-leaders/

Mark, J. J. (2023, November 20). Falling Star. World History Encyclopedia. https://www.worldhistory.org/article/2329/falling-star

Mark, J. J. (2024, January 19). Cheyenne Legends of the Buffalo. World History Encyclopedia. https://www.worldhistory.org/article/2353/cheyenne-legends-of-the-buffalo/

Matthews, A. S. (2022, February 2). Spirituality and Religious Beliefs of the Mi'kmaq. ArcGIS StoryMaps. https://storymaps.arcgis.com/stories/ee889ed588034218a63ce56971ebf820

McLeod, T. (2017). Hopi Prophecy—A Timeless Warning. Sacred Land. https://sacredland.org/hopi-prophecy

Millman, L. (1987). A Kayak Full of Ghosts. Capra Press.Native American Mythology. (2024). Twinkl.co.za. https://www.twinkl.co.za/teaching-wiki/native-american-mythology

Nair, N. (2022, October 5). Saquasohuh : The Blue Star Kachina. Mythlok. https://mythlok.com/saquasohuh

National Park Service. (2016). Sitting Bull - Little Bighorn Battlefield National Monument (U.S. National Park Service). Nps.gov. https://www.nps.gov/libi/learn/historyculture/sitting-bull.htm

Nordquist, R. (2019, May 4). Which of Your Favorite Stories are Actually Fables? ThoughtCo. https://www.thoughtco.com/what-is-a-fable-1690848

Pastore, R. T. (2016, October). Traditional Mi'kmaq (Micmac) Culture. Www.heritage.nf.ca. https://www.heritage.nf.ca/articles/indigenous/mikmaq-culture.php

Plains Indians - Cheyenne - Native Americans in Olden Times for Kids. (2019). Mrdonn.org. https://nativeamericans.mrdonn.org/plains/cheyenne.html

Ramirez, S. (2022, June 6). Wilma Mankiller Led as the First Woman Principal Chief of the Cherokee Nation. Smithsonian American Women's History. https://womenshistory.si.edu/blog/wilma-mankiller-led-first-woman-principal-chief-cherokee-nation

Reading Rockets. (n.d.). Native American Traditional Tales and Legends | Reading Rockets. Www.readingrockets.org. https://www.readingrockets.org/books-and-authors/booklists/american-indian-and-alaska-native-history-and-culture/native-american

Reed, J. (2024, March 13). The Life of Wilma Mankiller, First Woman to Serve as Principal Chief of the Cherokee Nation | National Trust for Historic Preservation. Savingplaces.org. https://savingplaces.org/guides/wilma-mankiller-first-woman-principal-chief-cherokee-nation

Sitting Bull (Tatanka Yotanka). (2017, August 2). UNHCR Central Europe. https://www.unhcr.org/ceu/9507-sitting-bull-tatanka-yotanka.html

Smith, S. (2015, September 16). The Legend of the Whispering Wind. Motherhood in Technicolor. https://www.motherhoodintechnicolor.com/the-legend-of-the-whispering-wind/

Stekel, P. (n.d.). Chief Seattle. HistoryNet. https://www.historynet.com/chief-seattle/

Summer, B. (2014, November 30). PPT - Mi'kmaq Creation Stories PowerPoint Presentation, free download - ID:7047989. SlideServe. https://www.slideserve.com/summer-barr/mi-kmaq-creation-stories

The Admin. (2024, February 24). Native American Tales: Unveiling Legends and Their Meanings. SOCIALSTUDIESHELP.COM. https://socialstudieshelp.com/native-american-tales-unveiling-legends-and-their-meanings/

The Hopi Origin Story | Native America. (n.d.). PBS LearningMedia. https://www.pbslearningmedia.org/resource/hopi-origin-story/hopi-origin-story/

Tribal Directory. (2016). Tlingit Raven Story. Tribaldirectory.com. https://tribaldirectory.com/information/tlingit-raven.html

Welker, G. (n.d.). How the Buffalo Hunt Began. Indians.org. https://indians.org/welker/buffhunt.htm

What is Folklore? – Social Sciences, Health, and Education Library (SSHEL) – U of I Library. (2019). Illinois.edu. https://www.library.illinois.edu/sshel/specialcollections/folklore/definition/

Wilson, L. (n.d.). Mankiller, Wilma Pearl | The Encyclopedia of Oklahoma History and Culture. Www.okhistory.org. https://www.okhistory.org/publications/enc/entry.php?entry=MA013

Made in the USA
Las Vegas, NV
26 November 2024

12749606R00059